SAW SOMETHING
now I'm SAYING
SOMETHING

What We Say and Do Matters in the Kingdom

By

Dr. Ginette A. Braziel, Ph.D.

SAW SOMETHING now I'm SAYING SOMETHING: What We Say and Do Matters in the Kingdom

By Dr. Ginette A. Braziel, Ph.D.

International Standard Book Number (ISBN) – 978-0-578-49165-3

Unless otherwise indicated, scripture is taken from The Holy Bible
Printed in the United States of America

Trademarks

All terms mentioned in this book that are known to be or are suspected of being trademarks or service marks have been appropriately capitalized. Use of a term in this book should not be regarded as affecting the validity of any trademark or service mark.

DEDICATION

This book is dedicated to my parents, Lucienne and Miredelle Alexandre, who went home to be with the Lord before they could see God call me into ministry, achieve my Doctoral degree and write this book. You were simply the best parents ever, love you! True love never dies!

ENDORSEMENTS

Suzan Lancaster - *Called to deliver this message, Dr. Braziel opens our eyes and compels us to see our environment through a different lens. "Saw Something now I'm Saying Something" demands that as kingdom builders we are called be accountable. Anointed by the Holy Spirit the author unfolds a story that must be told.*

Jasmine Demps *-Books are meant to move you and draw an emotion and "Saw Something now I'm Saying Something" brings out the emotion in me! Dr. Braziel's ability to draw you into the book with captivating examples with biblical reference is phenomenal!! A must read if you want to understand the inner workings of ministry.*

Crystal Foster *-The information that Dr. Ginette Braziel has so carefully written about will help all leaders understand the importance of Strong Holy Spirit led leadership. It's a subject that needed to be explored and exposed, so that we can all handle others with great care, leading with love. Thank you, Dr. Braziel, for your hard work and great effort in building up the Kingdom agenda.*

FOREWORD

By GOD

ACKNOWLEDGEMENT

First and foremost, I want to thank the lover of my soul, the one that first loved me, my Lord and Savior Jesus Christ: my inspiration, the one that gave me wisdom, knowledge and a measure of faith and the determination, and the courage to put my thoughts in writing.

I want to thank my friend and sister in Christ, Ms. Suzan Lancaster for pushing me, for encouraging me, and for believing in me and being the second set of eyes when I needed you. I love you girl, thank you for being on my team.

Thank you, Shanna Sarsin, for the cards and the push of inspiration you gave me. Tanasha, Dawn, Trina, Patricia, and Antoinette, thank you for your words of encouragement and prayers that covered me along the way.

And, last but not least, to Dr. LaVerne Adams, my book coach and editor, whose guidance and support let me know I didn't have to figure it out all by myself; and whose counsel and direction, awakened something in me to help me focus so that I could pour out what was in me and finish the course. I am grateful for your genius.

Thank you to all the leaders that challenged me in this area of leadership, it has pushed me to examine this area of leadership closer and shed some light on this particular subject in ministry to help others who are coming behind me to have a basic awareness of the things that go on in ministry that would otherwise take them by surprise and cause them to turn away in despair.

TABLE OF CONTENTS

INTRODUCTION

*T*his book is written for LEADERS, particularly leaders IN the Christian Church who have any level of AUTHORITY, to help us better understand that what we say and what we do matters and has a kingdom impact that will last throughout many generations. How leaders in authority perceive gifted and talented leaders under their leadership as rivals and a threat to their ministry, influences poor decision making.

As leaders, we must realize what you say matters and can be the difference between breaking yokes and changing a life or breaking a person spirit in a way that hinders their walk with God. This book is about awareness and survival in ministry. It's about being in a culture where you submit yourself to authority under a leadership that is called to equip you with knowledge and understanding for the purpose of carrying out the will of God and assist you in walking into your purpose and destiny. It's about facing facts and reality.

This book is about sharing my own personal experience and telling my truth. It's about bringing awareness to others, who may not fully understand what they are experiencing, nor can it be defined. This material is designed to let you know that resentment can come from someone who has a title that comes with power, that has the influence to help you fulfill your assignment.

It's about removing guilt from the one who has experienced this kind of treatment from a leader and encouraging them to keep their focus on the assignment, not the one in whom you are assigned. It's about no longer overlooking unacceptable behaviors that may cause you to abort your calling due to the damage poor impartation, but bringing them to the forefront for correction, conviction, and most of all, to set someone... free.

PURPOSE

Why this topic

God has given me this task and has prepared me to take any hits that come as a result of writing this book. I have been anointed to write on this topic and produce this book. Have you ever heard someone say things you despise or things that rubs you the wrong way? Well, it is these things that cause you to become truly passionate and you will not hesitate to speak on it in order to see change. While this is an important subject to speak on and should be an important one that we should strive to solve, bringing awareness and provoke change is necessary if you want to see a difference.For those of you who never heard this before, now you are aware and it's time for you to do what you can to make a difference, make your mark and impact change in this world! What is it that you are passionate about? What irritates you in a way that nothing else does? Well, if God is the author and finisher of your faith, then it must be God who placed this idea in you long before you were born. I believe God starts the thoughts that we believe. He created us for His good to accomplish His mission and vision on this earth.

As for me, I've always disliked seeing Christians treat other Christians badly. Don't get me wrong ... not that I mind the world treating Christians bad or others being treated bad because I most certainly don't like that either. I have heart for all people… period. When the world treats us bad for when we live as Christ taught, it's expected that we will suffer persecution, so we forgive them like Jesus who said "Father, forgive them for they know not what they do". As David said when he went through his trial, "if it was an enemy I would understand."

> **Psalm 55:12-14** - *For it was not an enemy that reproached me; then I could have borne it: neither was it he that hated me that did magnify himself against me; then I would have hid myself from him: But it was thou, a man mine equal, my guide, and mine acquaintance. We took sweet counsel together and walked unto the house of God in company.*

When I see Christians mistreat each other, my heart aches, because one of the first things we're taught and commanded as a Christians is to love and second is to love one another as you love yourself. **Mark 12:30-31** *"The second is this: 'Love your neighbor as yourself.' There is no commandment greater than these."* And also, in1 John 4:11*"Beloved, if God so loved us, we ought also to love one another."*

So, when resentment involves leaders, one can assume there is an underlying reason for it and must look at the root cause in the one doing the resenting. It becomes apparent that this person does not love themselves, or has some insecurities going on within themselves, and their true love cannot abound and is therefore incapable of giving real love to others.

Now let's take this to the next level. When Leaders do this to one another, it really breaks God's Heart because at this level of experience we should be seasoned in the faith and we should know better and do better and therefore set the example for the flock. Typically, when this happens there are some underlying issues that caused resentment in the first place. When we allow unresolved issues to run deep within, it's like the bad fruit of your own spirit, going against the fruit of the spirit.

Recently when I had to pick a topic for my dissertation while studying for my Ph.D. in Pastoral Ministry, this subject became highlighted for me but little did I know, God was setting me up. Sometimes you wonder why you are going through what you are going through and have to experience some harsh things in life. Well, this is my understanding of why... it's a set up for His glory. But what I didn't expect is that when I started to research the topic, I thought I would find lots of literature and material on this subject, but I didn't. I found that to be strange because we have so many wonderful and brilliant Christian authors out there who have written on just about every topic known to man. I saw a lot of information on resentment in the church but it always referenced a relationship between man and women and or marriage relationships but that was about it.

As I prayed and asked the Holy Spirit for guidance, I found that this was a topic that we didn't want to talk about or discuss in The Church because it has a bad connotation attached to it. Some things you just don't discuss or talk about because it's family business and is not to be discussed in or outside the Church. This was our little secret amongst us leaders. This topic exposes insecurities, weakness, bad behaviors, attitudes, frailness, and shows us the nature of who we really are. It also highlights and exposes the truth that we are not necessarily the person or the image we portray to the world or the people we think we are representative of in the church, television or on social media. Now is a good opportunity for us as leaders to take a deeper look at ourselves and take this time to get free and be better servants.

Resentment...what does that really mean? I've searched several dictionaries definitions and came up with a combination for each and formulated an explanation in my own words that I thought would help explain what it really means as it relates to this issue, or at least give leaders a comprehensive view of what it means to me.

Resentment means to be bitter from having been mistreated; building bad feelings or hard feelings against another individual. It means holding animosity, envy and jealousy or holding ill will against someone with a feeling of anger regarding someone or something unfair. It's a feeling of indignant displeasure regarding a wrong, an insult, or injury, or a feeling of dissatisfaction. Resentment is considered to be synonymous with anger, spite, and other similar emotions. While it may incorporate elements of these emotions, resentment is distinct from these emotions in several ways. Aside from sharing similar facial expressions, resentment and anger differ primarily in the way they are externally expressed. Anger results in aggressive behavior, used to avert or deal with a threat while resentment occurs once personal emotional injury has been sustained and is not expressed as aggressively or as openly. Resentment and spite also differ primarily in the way they are expressed. Resentment is unique in that it is almost exclusively internalized, where it can do further emotional and psychological damage to impact the person who resents as well as the person being resented. By contrast, spite is exclusively externalized, involving vindictive actions against a perceived, or actual, source of the wrong. Spiteful actions can stem from resentful feelings, however.

I would further assert that resentment is about relationships and the way we will feel about others and how they make us feel about ourselves. While relationships require some degree of commitment, in relationships where this resentful attitude exists, something has gone awry. Something has driven us to the point of resentment. While very few want to admit or discuss this topic, I believe this attitude of resentment to be very much alive and operating in the ministry.

Committing to a Leader/Follower relationship is something that evolves. It's not something that is instantly decided. After some consideration, I realized that resentment really has had a big effect on those who submit under the authority of someone who is a resentful leader. This becomes even more evident when addressing personal growth in ministry. This condition is compounded and contributes to poor decision making. Furthermore, this can negatively impact the entire ministry, including the intrinsic nature of the ministry and the church. It is critical that Christian Leaders learn to lead in a way without causing resentment to develop in those whom they serve. Furthermore, I believe it's crucial for us to examine our level of spirituality in order to bring about a change in this area.

This is the premise behind the story of Saul and David, 1st Samuel starting at the 16th Chapter. I found this story to be so relatable to situations that occur in some ministry contexts and even in which I have found myself. It's a sad story with a bittersweet ending; one that grieves the heart, and reaches to the core of the soul. Saul first encounters David when he couldn't sleep and was tormented by evil spirits because the hand of the Lord had departed from him. He was troubled deep in his soul. David was a warrior and a strong man who tended to sheep also played the harp, and the Lord was with him. He came when summoned by King Saul's court to see about such a man so troubled. He was asked to play the harp to remove those evil spirits and the music from David's harp would calm him. At first Saul loved David like a son because of what David could do for him. And, that's how the resentment relationship usually starts out. You have something to offer the Man or Women of God. Saul eventually took David on as his armor bearer recognizing that this one is special and I need to keep him close to me. All was well until something happened to change Saul's heart. David didn't change; he just wanted to continue to improve King Saul's quality of life. From the look of things, Saul allowed jealously and envy to creep into his heart causing this relationship that was once so great and fruitful, to become tainted. It stands to reason though because Saul, who had been rejected by God as King, now becomes resentful of David, whom God had chosen to be next King. Knowing that Saul had a love for David at one time, one would question how a relationship that seemed so right could go so wrong.

It is important to note that David slew Goliath and Saul put him over his men in charge the wars and battles because he trusted David. The scripture makes it clear that Saul had become quite disturbed by the achievements of David, creating spiritual turmoil in Saul. It is important to recognize that David did not assign himself these duties and responsibilities. He was appointed by and submitted to Saul's leadership. One has to assume that David wanted to do the best job at what he was given by his leader. It becomes increasingly clear that King Saul's spirituality was out of balance, and his resentment of David eventually became the cause of Saul's poor decision making. Although, David was already playing the harp for him, when he came back from killing Goliath, Saul did not even know who he was. Saul loved David, but soon saw him as a threat and a rival to his kingdom. David was just being David. The gift and the talents that David possessed made Saul angry in his Spirit, and he allowed his weaknesses to consume him which severely affected his decision making. It is when the selfishness and jealously is allowed to fester that it consequently destroyed a good relationship.

Jealousy

Chad Johnson (2010) states that "jealousy is as cruel as the grave". Jealousy and resentment walk side by side, and even go hand in hand because they are similar in definition. David merely wanted to serve Saul and was waiting on God's guidance and timing, to become ruler of the kingdom. On one occasion when David came in from battle, the people began to praise him more than Saul. David didn't praise himself -- the people did. In John 14:11-13, Jesus said "greater works shall you do". If I may paraphrase this verse of scripture, David did greater works and Saul could not take it. This was indeed the Hand of God turning the hearts of the people of Israel to their new King. If Saul had only been in the right place with God, and his spirituality was strong, he would have been prepared for this to occur in David's life and submit to the divine will of God. The key focus here is being "right with God". If I can be honest and say, a lot of leaders are not right with God. There are leaders that may look spiritual and even act spiritual but that doesn't mean they are right with God. As a leader, Saul should have been proud of the greater works done by David and grateful for all the blessings David brought into his life. What makes this even sadder is that David just wanted to please Saul. He was obedient to Saul's requests even when it put him in harm's way where his life could have been taken. Some leaders can allow themselves to be so bitter that they are willing to wipe out someone's life just for their own selfish satisfaction. But the numerous attempts for Saul to try to kill David can also represent the reality for some of today's ministry relationships. Resentful leaders will try to kill a person's spirit by suppressing them just so they can come in line with them. And although they desire to use the gift and talents that God has placed in the people they lead, some may even go as far as putting them in harm's way. Saul desperately tried to destroy David, and he did whatever it took, because he saw David as threat to his power. But isn't that the same game that happens in the ministry with leaders in authority who become threatened by the gifts they see in those under their authority. And instead of nurturing that gift and seeing those talents go forth for the edification of the ministry and the kingdom of God, because of personal insecurities, they sometimes seek to destroy the very talents that they are charged to help develop and nurture. We know God is certainly not pleased with this! That's not God, that's the enemy doing his best work. And the question becomes what are we gonna' do about it?

Thankfully David was wise, and he acted and behaved wisely and removed himself from the presence of Saul. Likewise, leaders get angry and wonder why we lose good servants and members in our ministry. Saul lost his mind at times, just like some of us, when things don't go our way. It must be noted that many leaders do forget the call on their lives, and all spiritual senses goes straight out the window, leaving the flesh in charge and the enemy in control. He told David in I Samuel 24:20 that surely, he would be king and asked for mercy. Saul tried to kill David again and again. This sounds familiar because even after they have left the confines of some leader's ministry and presence, these leaders are still trying to kill them again, and again and again. This bears repeating. Saul wanted to literally kill David just as some leaders literally try to kill a person's spirit and wound their soul and extinguish the things that God created in them. And some won't stop until they do. And just like Saul eventually fell on his own sword, if leaders continue to act in such an unacceptable manner that is not pleasing to God, their destruction is inevitable. It would behoove you to be careful because just like Saul, you will also be in a battle and have to fall on your own sword. But there are some leaders that would rather fall on their own sword than to have to face the mistakes and enemies made through past behaviors. Saul may have been anointed as King, but he still was judged for his sin against God and David. As Leaders, we may be in a position of authority, but we still have a higher authority to answer to as well, and we will be judged harder in the end. We will all have to give account to God for the harsh deeds and treatment of his people whom He put under our care to watch, train, nurture, rebuke, and most importantly to show God's love. It is critical to understand that you cannot treat the people of God wrong and think that there will be no consequences. No matter what title or position you hold, you didn't choose yourself, you were chosen by God. Well, let me also state that there are some who chose themselves but that's another story and you all know what I mean by that... enough said. One more thought about the consequences before I move on which is food for thought. Remember the dreams God showed you as a leader in the beginning of your journey, maybe a larger church, a huge congregation, and financial wealth that he was going to bless you with, that just hasn't come to pass yet. And do you remember that some of your spiritual son and daughters even prophesied to you what God told them and show them when they entered your ministry which brought confirmation to you. Their presence in your ministry shifted the ministry to a new level and you could taste and see the promise starting to come to pass.

Well, it is important to remember that there are conditions to the promise. For example, if God gives you more resources, can you handle it and treat it with care? Well, you may want to consider how are you doing with what you already have been charged with. And when God sends someone into the ministry to bless you, do you recognize that they are your blessing and part of the promise? Well then, enough said on this matter! SELAH, yes, you may want to think on these things.

DEFINITIONS

I thought it would be good if start out by sharing a few definitions for you refer to and reflect on during the course of your reading. These were some definitions I gathered from my readings and research that I thought would be helpful.

Jealousy

Jealousy is defined as resentment against a rival, a person enjoying success or advantage, etc., or against another's success or advantages itself.

Leadership

Leaders can be described in many ways, but most uphold the characteristics of the word Leadership in order to be identified as a leader. Leadership is the art of influencing and getting others to do something you want and inspiring individuals to perform a common mission. It is further defined as the power or ability to lead other people. Being in a position as a leader of a group or organization, and leading others includes having authority over others. The position or function of a leader is a person who guides or directs a group. Leaders help themselves and others to do the right things. They set direction, build an inspiring vision, and create something new. Leadership is about mapping out where you need to go in order to "win" as a team or an organization; which can be dynamic, exciting, and inspiring. Yet, while leaders set the direction, they must also use management skills to guide their people to the right destination, in a meaningful and efficient way. True leadership creates a future and an inspiring vision for those being led. It motivates and inspires people to engage with a vision of hope to see them doing greater things. Those in leadership are charged with coaching and building a team, so that it is more effective at achieving the vision. Leadership brings together skills to do all things required to accomplish the mission or task.

Spirituality

Spirituality is a broad concept with room for many perspectives. In general, it includes a sense of connection to something bigger than us, and it typically involves a search for meaning in life. And as such, it is a universal human experience — something that touches us all. (Merriam-Webster).

Decision-Making and Leadership

Decision making takes into account a variety of things in the process of determining an outcome. I believe that there are a variety of influences that impact how an individual makes decisions. Influencing factors might include education, experience, culture, religion, gender, attitude, and the environment. Vroom and Yetton (1973).

Spiritually Grounded

This person is saved, a believer, and a student of the word. It's their daily bread. A spiritually grounded individual sets the example for others. They are influencers and one of good character. They stand on the principle of holiness and righteousness, their title doesn't have to be mentioned, it's known by the way they carry themselves and treat others. When in a position of leadership people can look to them for guidance directions. They are those who make others feel safe and assured in their presence or under their leadership. It's an individual who is well balanced in temper and behavior. It is one who makes sound and sensible decisions, considering all others, and a selfless individual. This person is a great manager of stress and stressful situations, they react accordingly and exhibits self- control and considered as one that doesn't keep score but prays for the positive outcome. They are a peace maker in every aspect choose peace over being right. They show love to all even when it's not reciprocated. They love God with all their, heart mind and soul. Stand in the posture and thought process of "what would Jesus do?" (WWJD). They are confident that there is no situation that God can't handle so they stay out panic mode and just pray, believe, hope and trust God.

A quick exert from my research studies

The goal of my research was to hear from the leaders in authority in their own words and to allow them to explain how leaders sometimes perceive those who are gifted and talented under their leadership as rivals and a threat to their ministry. The study analyzes how the leader's view of these gifts, and in some instances influenced poor decision making. Moreover, the study looks at whether leaders believe that their spirituality influences the decisions they make in their roles as leaders.

How spirituality influences the decision-making of Leaders considered to be in higher positions and in authority in the Church are in a unique position to influence in the decision-making process and in many individual's lives. Understanding more about how they make their decisions could shed light on the decision-making process itself and give us a better understanding of how to prevent leaders from falling into a pattern of resentment. Additionally, I believe that your leadership style is directly influenced by your spirituality.

Additionally, what leaders say and do matters and have a lasting impact. So, if you are a leader, the question remains: if you understand that spirituality plays a big role in a leader's decision-making process, where are you spiritually?

OBSERVATION ONE

Resentment

Resentment breeds all these other actions I'm portraying in the book. When resentment kicks in these topics are what I heard leaders say and saw them do over my almost 20 years of committed ministry. This is merely my observation and my experience in the area of leadership. I have also been a product of being resented in leadership, so I have firsthand experience, so I'm not going by what I heard, I'm going by what I know to be true. This is my truth of what I've lived and walked through over the years. The thing is that I still respect and love each one of the leaders I've served under; they were very powerful and anointed men and women of God. They help shaped me as a leader, with all the good bad and the ugly that I've experienced. It was good that I was afflicted; it made me better not bitter. I received so much wisdom and knowledge that only experience can teach. Now that I'm a leader, I'm trying to take all my experiences and what I've learned from other leaders of what to do and what not to do, and try to do it better and be the difference. I know we all fall short of the glory. I'm working out my own salvation daily. My objective here is not to condemn or judge but to bring awareness to leaders. And don't be surprised, because if you're honest with yourself, you may find a little bit of you in some of these Observations. Now I do think we say a lot of stuff as leaders that really affects and infects the body of Christ and we really don't realize it has a lasting impact and a lasting impression on the people of God. Remember, leaders who raise up other leaders and the oil falls down from the beard, pure or tainted it's going to fall. Now to read the content, may help us to look at ourselves differently and self-reflect to be better leaders that God may continue to get the glory and be glorified through our lives.

Resentment has become a common theme in the church causing it to gain the attention of some leadership cultures. I believe that a culture exists that has had the experience of being a part of this group of gifted but resented servants: a group that is mistreated solely because of gifts and talents. It is because this culture exists, that we must shine a light on it and investigate the causes and effects. No longer can we pretend that it doesn't exist. Being resented, in my opinion, can be abusive in its nature and unaddressed fosters a negative environment. Where this culture exists leaders must be made aware, especially the leader in question. In the situations in which this occurs, we hope that spirituality will kick in for awareness sake when making decisions concerning others in the body of Christ. In cases where there is no quality of thought in their spirituality, no compassion for others or empathy, leaders must allow themselves to understand an individual and celebrate a gift before applying an external behavior that can be detrimental to the individual, the ministry, or organization in the end. The root of the word spirituality is spirit, and our spirits must be right to connect with the mind of God.

What is at the root of the term Resentment is "to resent", which is to use a feeling to show displeasure or indignation to a person by an act or a remark from a sense to injure and insult one (Wikipedia). When used in this manner it shows that one must internalize a true dislike of an individual to feel this way. Once this is internalized, the act of displeasure exists. It is then that the "something" that you just don't like about someone "the disconnection" begins to take a root. Typically, these feeling will co-exist with the spirit of jealousy towards one. This often followed by the behavior of the leader becoming inappropriate. This behavior can begin with the insult, shunning, ignoring, or displaying all types of unacceptable behavior. This creates an atmosphere within the church where the leaders with gifts and talents cannot thrive.

All spirituality goes out the window, and the ministry becomes void of the Holy Spirit. However, when healthy spirituality is present, leaders often want to create a spirit of harmony, love and cooperation within a church. This can in turn, create a positive atmosphere where leaders are creative with their gifts and talents. This environment fosters high motivation, self-driven attitude, and a desire to work hard in ministry and support their leadership in authority. The leaders that have the authority to make decisions benefit from the positive atmosphere and of this proves to be for the good of the Church and the Ministry. Such an environment may often be referred to as the Kingdom of God and His plan being executed and fulfilled on earth, and the spiritual morale of the leaders in the church is high. Similarly, everyone is on one accord working towards the mission and the vision of the church. This creates a spirit of excellence at work. It also helps to create the same type of environment where everyone has a common focus and a common goal to do the will of God. Guillory (1997) believes collaboration within groups is possible only when there is a spiritual connection between the members of the group who share a similar mission or goal. He provides several additional characteristics, which include harmony, interconnectedness, and oneness, being on one accord.

Collaborative external communities outside the four walls of the church such as the workplace and Church communities share some of the same characteristics that promote spirituality in either place. Collaborative communities are environments where there is a close sense of community or spirituality. While the term spirituality may not be used to describe a specific type of activity, individual, or even management style, it is indeed a more "spiritual" environment that many attempts to achieve in the workplace, but without specifically using the term.

Benefiel (2003) believes a company's performance can be positively impacted by spirituality. In other we are better together, two are better than one, this not only goes for a company, but it applies to any organization and especially the church.

Spirituality can be difficult to define. Fry (2003). In order to embrace spirituality, one must understand that love, humility, truth, honesty, compassion, trust, vision, integrity, are a few of the words used to describe spirituality. However, the qualities that terms such as compassion, love, truth, humility, trust, and integrity embody are a part of the church's vocabulary and especially vision. The bible says write the vision and make it plain. Such is the mission of the church leaders. (Habakkuk Chapter 2).

I thought I would bring into this book, a little bit of talk about religion, as it may pertain to spirituality. I hear people of the faith describe some resentful behaviors as religion. This leads one to analyze the meaning of such a description. This body of research attempts to compare and explain the meaning of resentment being described as religion.

Resentment in the area of Christian Leadership is typically not openly spoken of especially as it pertains to any writings or Literature about the Church. Most often when you see resentment in leadership it is addressed in scholarly research or it is in reference to marital relationships or workplace relationships. I read many books on the Church Leadership, and it seems very obvious that Church and the Church Leaders may not care to discuss this topic very much, due to the lack of available literature and materials on this topic. Now I must say, some churches may broach this subject, but it's probably more than likely taught inside of the church during leadership training and discussed only when necessary. I understand that some leaders think that it exposes the body of Christ and Church leaders and could possibly air out the dirty laundry of the ministry. That is why discussing this topic may make some leaders feel uncomfortable, because it forces them honestly reflect on their behaviors which is ok, because that discomfort is an opportunity for the leader to take a good look at themselves! Not to mention the fact that it's no fun dying to the flesh, which is something that is very difficult to do. Selah. Now the real issue is that unless we confront or examine problems in the Church head-on, and put all the facts on the table for discussion, we can never make the Kingdom of God and the church as great as God intended it to be here on earth as it is in heaven. As a reminder Christ loved the church and gave himself for it! *Ephesians 5:26-27- That he might sanctify and cleanse it with the washing of water by the word, that he might present it to himself a glorious church, not having spot, or wrinkle, or any such thing; but that it should be holy and without blemish.* Jesus is coming back, you know! We will never become the people that God calls us to be by overlooking or dismissing these issues. If this behavior is not addressed, we will fail at continuing to build upon the word of God and what Christ has commanded and left for us to do. We cannot continue to make disciples and build and stir up the gifts in the body of Christ if we don't recognize and call out that which is wrong and make every attempt and effort to make it right and therefore pleasing to God.

Let's start our journey by defining and gaining a deeper understanding into Christian Leadership, Church management and the importance of deepening your own spirituality. Definitions of leadership and management vary widely. It is difficult to pin down one definition that succinctly defines traditional leadership and management theory, especially in the Church. Spirituality is not a type of leadership style; it's a quality that influences how people lead and their style of how they are led to behave.

I believe the real challenge here is helping leaders to recognize and understand the true depth of their spirituality and how it influences their decisions. What we must further understand is the important role this plays in becoming better leaders. Fry (2003) describes the characteristics of spirituality such as love, truth, honesty, trust, vision, humility, and integrity in describing a spiritual leader. However, we cannot force people to integrate these qualities into their leadership.

One might note that leaders who embrace these attributes find that they are more successful in the Kingdom building. In other words, your actions without any feelings connected, has nothing to do with spirituality. Fry (2003) also suggests that spirituality is a way of leading others, inspiring them, and helping them to achieve their fullest potential.

True spirituality involves a completely different method of thinking and a totally different mindset rather than just going through the motions. Senior leaders charged with leading others must step up and take their rightful place, in order for this to be effective within the church, after all, we lead by example. We must adopt a deeper level of spirituality within the church as a lifestyle in which we should live and practice daily. This will require the transformation of people and mindsets, which to be sure, will not happen overnight. This will involve a process to get the desired but necessary results. Deal (1995) believes that leading with the heart and soul can be used as a way to empower people. So why not use this same principle and bring it into the realm of the Church. It goes without saying that Leaders should adopt a deep spiritual approach when attempting to lead others in the Church. While success is not guaranteed with this approach, it is definitely worth the effort. If the leadership within a Church could recognize the importance of heightened spirituality and how it impacts one's performance, this benefit alone would make a difference in the church.

I believe without a shadow of a doubt that a mandated process for spiritual growth and development in leaders could be the key to success when it comes to leading people effectively. It is important to note that people respond positively to the spiritually based leadership of those called to lead. Dreher (1996) believes that great leaders inspire us with a vision of further possibilities. This is so because they share their vision and challenge us reach our potential and encourage us thrive, simply because they have already modeled much of the same.

Scriptures

Colossians 3:8-13 - *"But now you must also rid yourselves of all such things as these: anger, rage, malice, slander, and filthy language from your lips. ⁹ Do not lie to each other, since you have taken off your old self with its practices ¹⁰ and have put on the new self, which is being renewed in knowledge in the image of its Creator. ¹¹ Here there is no Gentile or Jew, circumcised or uncircumcised, barbarian, Scythian, slave or free, but Christ is all, and is in all.¹² Therefore, as God's chosen people, holy and dearly loved, clothe yourselves with compassion, kindness, humility, gentleness and patience. ¹³ Bear with each other and forgive one another if any of you has a grievance against someone. Forgive as the Lord forgave you."*

Prayer

Oh, my heavenly Father, I acknowledge my sin, because I know when I sin it's against you and you alone. I am taking ownership and acknowledging that I've held resentment and bitterness against others that you have place under my authority. I confess this sin and ask you to forgive me. Please remind and convict me Lord, so that I may not hold any more resentment towards anyone, but rather to love others. Father, I ask you to also forgive those that may have spoken evil towards me for my actions. Help us to reconcile and make peace that we make live in a way that's pleasing to you. Thank You for hearing and answering my prayer. In Jesus' Holy Name, Amen.

OBSERVATION TWO

Now, Who Made You God?

"*I am the LORD, and there is no other; apart from me there is no God. I will strengthen you, though you have not acknowledged me,* (Isaiah 45:5 NIV). YOU, oh Lord are the Lord God and there is no other God! Now ponder that for just a minute! There are times, when a leader gets in a position of authority, and quickly forgets the ladder that they came up on, or even the hardship endured that wasn't pleasant. Yes, how soon we forget! Now for some the ladder may have been pretty easy because you came through the family and through succession. In other words, you were cared for nurtured and groomed for the position. And for others you just came by the calling and the leading of the Holy Spirit and call of God. I won't get on the topic of privilege and arrogance that's another story for another day. And there are those who are sent, and there are those who just went. Where in this process do we begin to treat people as if we own them? Where does that come from? What is the root cause of this behavior? There are some people who get in positions that they create themselves just so they can have authority over others. Then when they get in authority, they abuse that authority and power, simply because they are not use to that much influence over others. Some may have never been in a leadership role. So, the first rule of thumb in the church is to understand that leaders do not own the people that they have authority over. The people belong to God. You didn't create them. God created them male and female and blessed them. And he named them "mankind" when they were created. (Genesis 5:2). So ask yourself, is this how we treat the things of God? If you cannot answer positively, you need a reality check. People under our authority are a gift to body of Christ. They have a choice and free will to obey God and to sit under our authority and let us lead them. They don't have to be there, and they can come and go as they please. However, our job as leaders is to guide them, teach them, nurture them, chasten and correct them as needed. We should teach them to serve and submit to authority and to honor those that are in leadership. But we should be a good example and develop them to the point of where they want to enjoy being a part of the assembly that God has led them to. I heard a Pastor say during his sermon, "if you don't know how to handle them with care, as sure as God has led them to you, he will lead them away from you."

Somehow, we tend to get that master and slave mentality as if they should do whatever they are told, wrong or right. Well, needless to say it just doesn't always work that way. This is especially when you have a carnal attitude and mindset that you want them to follow and satisfy your fleshly desires that are not of God. What you're actually saying is follow me and not follow Christ. Bottom line they should follow you as you follow Christ. Not follow you as you follow your flesh or feelings. Your actions should be Bible based and not humiliating or degrading to the individual. Check yourself before you act, and think what would Jesus do? (WWJD) Even when Judas had planned Jesus demise at the Last

Supper, Jesus could have exposed him for this unthinkable act of betrayal but instead, Jesus said to the Twelve disciple, whose feet He had washed, "You are clean," the Lord had specified an exception by His after remark, "but not all. By doing this Jesus acknowledged that he knew that He would be betrayed by Judas, but even then, He did not submit to his flesh. What Jesus is teaching us here is that we must always think before we react. The people should not have to submit to the foolishness of your flesh. A leader at this point needs to search themselves and find out what underlying issues that they have.

Facing unresolved issues is the best way to get to the root of it and get some deliverance from it. It's available to all, you just need to seek guidance from other "mature, respectable and responsible leaders". Please remember that God trusted you with his sheep and expects you to be a good shepherd. And contrary to popular belief, "ALL" sheep ain't dumb. They follow you because they choose to, they also see something in your gift talents and abilities that they admire and desire to glean from. They want to learn how to walk in their purpose and destiny designed for their lives. To be honest that's the only reason some of them stick around as long as they do. Consequently, because of you are charismatic, gifted and knowledgeable and can sing a little bit. Yes, those gifts that you have obtained over the years, people tend to follow despite an ugly disposition towards them...but not for long. The sad truth is when leaders are gifted in the body of Christ, we give them permission to operate in their brokenness, and that's not good. Your brokenness can get lead the sheep to slaughter! Thank God our gift is given without repentance. Where would some of us be without the amazing grace of

God? Please remember these people are human and not actual sheep in a pasture. So, I am pleading with you to do a self-examination of how you're treating your folks. Yes, you will have some good days and yes you have some bad days where you will lash out unexpectedly because of whatever is going on in your own life. Or you may experience frustration because of their behavior and that's understandable. None of us are perfect, but we must surrender and allow spirit of God to work in us. *Psalm 138:8 The LORD will perfect that which concerns me; Your mercy, O LORD, endures forever; Do not forsake the works of Your hands.* Yes, God will perfect what concerns us, but we must stay in prayer and in God's Presence. But if your pattern of unacceptable behavior continues, then what I'm saying here is that you need to change. Remember, you are not God, you are only a keeper of his sheep and the appointed Shepherd submitted to God the Chief Shepherd. SELAH.

 **Scriptures**

1st Thessalonians 2:4 – *"Instead, we speak as those approved by God to be entrusted with the gospel, not in order to please men but God, who examines our hearts. 1st Corinthians 10:33 just as I try to please everyone in all I do. For I am not seeking my own good, but the good of many, that they may be saved."*

Prayer

Father forgive me if I have not treated your sheep in good faith. You entrusted me with them as their shepherd, now please help me to do better and be more aware of, and cautious of, what I'm saying and doing at all times. Thank you restoring your trust in me. Help me to not bleed on the sheep with my mess as I shepherd them to help them find their purpose and destiny. Create in me a clean heart and fix my brokenness. In Jesus name I pray. Amen.

OBSERVATION THREE

Is it a Pulpit or a Just a Pit?

I s it a sacred altar, or the pit in which Joseph was thrown in by his brothers? I 'm confused. Leaders, please stop going off over the Pulpit, airing out your dirty laundry. Stop it, just stop it! That's right! Please stop sharing those deceptive dysfunctional things that lies in your heart. Jeremiah 17:9 says *"the heart is deceitful above all things, and desperately sick; who can understand it."* (ESV) The pulpit is not the platform for you to let your flesh loose to attack and assault the people of God with your words. The pulpit is defined as an elevated platform or high reading desk used in preaching or conducting a worship service. In a preaching profession and a preaching posture and or position, a platform is a raised structure in a church, from which the sermon and the "Good News" is delivered and the service is conducted. It is not good news when you "cut up" like that.

This is the most cowardly move I ever seen from a leader other than communicating foolishly on social media. Remember as we discussed previously? The people are not yours you don't own them. God allows them to come into your ministry for you to train them, equip them, prune them, prepare them and send some them out to build the kingdom of God and continue to the work of God! A pulpit is designed to pull people out of the pit and out of the hands of the enemy. But some leaders have a tendency to use this as a personal platform to release their frustration and personal feelings that pulls the people into a pit. Why do we have a tendency to spill out what whatever someone has done to you or how someone made you feel to discuss it over the Pulpit? By doing this, you have defiled the altar of God and have disrespected what God deems Holy. One day you say the pulpit is sacred and in the next breath you are saying cruel and evil things across it to get back at someone in the church most of the time. Some leaders operate with a "get back" spirit. May that spirit of "get back" be broken off of you, in Jesus' name.

If a church member or another leader in the church does something wrong or disrespected you, which we know will eventually happen, (and if it hasn't happened yet, it's going to happen, just keep on leading), and you have already rebuked them privately so why do you still need to get them back even the more. Your flesh is not quite satisfied doing it God's way, so now you start rebuking them publicly. You don't seem to be satisfied until you have crushed their spirit or send them running out of the doors of the church. Then you get upset because they left, and you say that they can't take rebuke. Well, what I think you meant to say is, they can't take verbal and emotional abuse, that is beyond normal spiritual chastening. This is an unfortunate circumstance when something so sacred and tainted with the weakness of the flesh. Then the blood is on your hands when you try to kill the very thing that God have entrusted you with! And is it any wonder why your Church is not growing, or it has become a revolving door? This may be because God can't trust you with the ones you have, so why would he trust you with more to damage and corrupt. It's time to stop being cowards. If you have something to say to an individual, pull them aside or in your office and discuss the matter as the bible exhorts. This is called being mature as leader! If you can't do this then you need to ask God to save you from you, and deliver you from yourself! We do so much damage to the body of Christ when we bring our flesh and mess to the Pulpit. This also puts the person you are trying to target at a disadvantage, because you know they are not going to say anything while you are supposed to be preaching the gospel at the sacred altar and stand on Holy ground. So be careful because you may run into the wrong person that is carnal minded and out of frustration, leap on you one day.

And, don't start using church jargon when confronted. The first thing we hear is "I wasn't talking about you, that's just my message, it could be for anybody." The people already know that's a good game. We already have had too many spiritual fatalities in church. We need the church to be a safe place a place of restoration, hope, and salvation. Come on leaders let's do better. Your words coming over the pulpit can be fatal to the body. So, let's all come out of the "pit" and let love abound.

Scriptures

Malachi 1:7 - "You have shown contempt by offering defiled sacrifices on my altar. "Then you ask, 'How have we defiled the sacrifices?' "You defile them by saying the altar of the LORD deserves no respect.

Ezekiel 44:16 - "They shall enter my sanctuary; they shall come near to My table to minister to Me and keep My charge."

Prayer

Father, when I approach your sacred place and your Holy Altar, help me to control my emotions and feeling. Set me aside in a way that I can get out of behaviors that are not pleasing to you. Help me to bring my flesh under subjection and focus on the word you have given me to speak behind your sacred desk. Forgive me for disrespecting that which you deem Holy and for releasing unholy fruit into the atmosphere of the Church, and over your people, giving way to the enemy into your house. In Jesus Name I pray. Amen.

OBSERVATION FOUR

The Number of Years in Ministry Does Not Equal Maturity in Ministry

Have you ever run into Leaders that have been in ministry a long time, I mean twenty plus years? You saw them on television they been on radio and they are highly respected and sought after, and you yourself grew to respect them as well over the years. Now years later you get to serve in their ministry under their leadership, and you're getting the opportunity to learn about the ministry and who they are as a leader. Because you look up to them as mentors and seasoned in the faith, you pay close attention to what they say as well as what they do, and you may become puzzled or even slightly confused. I have seen this a few times on my ministry journey. The first time I was a bit devastated. But as I have matured and walked in ministry, I've since learned that this is a common behavior amongst some of the leaders. You think to yourself; this person has been in ministry for a long time, but their behavior, attitude, title, and the way they conduct themselves in the ministry, just don't match up. Then you start to notice that they do really immature things that you would expect babes in Christ to do. And you see that they also do things that negatively influence the souls under their care and the Body of Christ. I've seen leaders that talk about everybody, and I mean everybody in the Church, including all their leaders, and anybody they know or meet! Something is wrong with everybody but them, and they will gossip to anybody that will listen and if you're not careful they will drag you into talking about people too! Sometimes when you find yourself listening to them, trying to respect their authority, and not be disrespectful and rude and cut them off, so you just listen. These types of leaders always want you to co-sign to what they are saying, and if you don't then they will leave you alone, mistreat you, or stop speaking to you. Then, they go get somebody that will agree to everything they are saying and start talking about you! I've seen some spread lies on others so they can "be right", when they know they are dead wrong and just don't want to admit it. But the thing is that you have got to be wise. Wisdom will tell you if they are talking about everybody, believe me when you ain't around, they are talking about you! It doesn't matter how close you walk with them you may even be their assistant or armor bearer. As a matter of fact, some of them carry themselves in a very mature way, being responsible in the Body of Christ. They understand the charge and the call. But this type of leader can potentially be dangerous because they can become abusive. They can hurt people by abusing their authority to get their thrills to feel like they are in charge and to feel good about themselves.

You may be surprised and think to yourself, "By now they should be past that because we all go through growing pains and stages of maturity. You think they should be more mature because of their titles and what it represents, but let me tell you a little secret, I've learned titles can be given prematurely and some leaders are trying to catch up with their titles, what I call a slip through the system. Then you see God raising up a younger generation that have sons and daughters under their leadership and we condemn them by saying they are too young to be spiritual Mothers and Fathers in the Gospel. But you are older, and you carry yourself with so much immaturity and your actions expose you. I said all that to say, get your character, attitude and spirit right before you pass judgment on others. You have been in ministry too long to still be acting like this. You know who you are. So, leaders examine yourself, and stop saying "I've been in ministry twenty plus years" because it's really embarrassing when your years don't line up with your actions and behavior. Like I said in the title ministry years does not always equal maturity in ministry.

Scriptures

Ephesians 4:13-15 – *"Until we all attain to the unity of the faith, and of the knowledge of the Son of God, to a mature man, to the measure of the stature which belongs to the fullness of Christ. As a result, we are no longer to be children, tossed here and there by waves and carried about by every wind of doctrine, by the trickery of men, by craftiness in deceitful scheming; but speaking the truth in love, we are to grow up in all aspects into Him who is the head, even Christ."*

1 Corinthians 13:11-*"When I was a child, I spake as a child, I understood as a child, I thought as a child: but when I became a man, I put away childish things."*

Prayer

Father I know my ways have not pleased you, and the example that I have set for others in the ministry may have not been satisfactory. Help me to get out of my flesh and put away my childish ways and behavior. Forgive me and please help me to watch my tongue and keep from gossiping and speaking the things I shouldn't speak about others. Fill every void in me that I might be made whole. Help me to work on my insecurities and building good character. In Jesus Name I pray, Amen.

OBSERVATION FIVE

When the Anointing Has Left the Building

Discernment is key. Always! Whatever you do in your prayer closet make sure you ask God for discernment. I have seen people with great voices sing, and people go wild. And yet something seems to be or little off in the atmosphere. I have seen preachers preach a good word; their gifts and talents are in full force the charisma is working, the show was real good, but something is missing! People are leaving the same way they came, and very few are getting saved for real. And what's even worse is that it seems like nobody's getting set free. I repeat, people are leaving out the same way they came in. You know why – because the anointing has left the building. As leaders we must understand how difficult it is to help people get delivered from stuff that we ourselves haven't been delivered from, especially when we are still dealing with things going on in our flesh. That's why your discernment in the body of Christ is crucial for yourself and the people. It may all be entertaining, but at the end of the day, you feel like you've wasted two to three hours of your life in an unfruitful service. I believe that God's Presence will leave a church due to disobedience of the leader. Leaders, if God give you a task and a mandate for your Church, God will also give you instructions for how your church should operate. If you allow someone to come in that God didn't authorize to take over your pulpit, or release something foul in your atmosphere, or disobey the original orders given by God for the church, you can expect a negative shift or change in the atmosphere.

Consequently, that anointed place will no longer be sacred to God and the anointing will just leave the building. The definition of a true anointing is found in Isaiah 10:27, *"And it shall come to pass in that day, that his burden shall be taken away from off thy shoulder, and his yoke from off thy neck, and the yoke shall be destroyed because of the anointing."* When I speak of the anointing, it's that spiritual essence that hovers over the atmosphere, where people are so touched that they will cry and don't know why they're crying. Under that kind of anointing, people will wail and travail, people will lay prostrate and folks will begin to speak in tongues and other will prophesy, and deliverance and healing takes place burdens are lifted souls are saved. That's the kind of anointing is what I'm referring to. Yes, you will still preach and teach in that atmosphere and sing and praise but the prophets and the discerners can call out that which is missing in that place. Many times, what the people think is a move of God is just a move of gifts and talents, which are without repentance. They will operate on their own. Now, the gifts of God are irrevocable. It's the level of operation that you should be concerned about and in this atmosphere of God the enemy hover in the church too. Those things I mentioned is the previous paragraph is what we want to see occur to make an impact in the kingdom. That's when you know God's anointing is present in your house. I have been in places where it seemed like the people no longer feared or reverence the anointing of God. Psalm 111:10 says *"The fear of the Lord is the beginning of wisdom; all those who practice it have a good understanding. His praise endures forever!"*

Just as the gifts of God are irrevocable, so is the anointing of God. How are you exercising your gift and the anointing God has placed on your life? Are you careless with such a precious gift? So, when you hear someone speaking of the church or a particular person who they say has lost the anointing, what they're really saying is that the person is not operating in the Spirit like they had before and that something seems to be missing. So, could it be possible to NOT be in church ministry and still have the anointing? The anointing is there, but sin and the anointing just don't mix, like vinegar and oil in the same cup that can't connect or join together as one. There is a separation, and they separate themselves from each other. 1 John 2:27 ESV says, *"But as for you, the anointing (the sacred appointment, the unction) which you received from Him abides [permanently] in you."* So, what I'm saying is that it's in you, but you have allowed sin, fear, condemnation or doubt to subdue the gift. Have you given into those wiles of the enemy? And now it seems like you have lost the gift. Could it be that what happens is that the person does not lose the gift, but they simply lose the confidence to function in that gift? The confidence to go boldly the heavenly Father is stolen by the enemy. Therefore, without faith they are limited in functioning in that gift or anointing. This is when you have to search and seek wisdom from God. The prophet Daniel explains that all wisdom comes from God as he writes, *"Blessed be the name of God forever and ever, to whom belong wisdom and might."* (Daniel 2:20). May the conviction of the spirit have its way, so that you can be better for the Kingdom of God. I'd say that conviction of sin and the feeling of not using the gift is good, if it allows you to repent and go back to God. But there are some who continue to function in the gifts within extreme faith, without any repentance. Thereby they are abusing the gifting that God has placed in them. At no point should you allow the enemy to hijack your gift or the anointing God has placed in you by bringing guilt and condemnation. And again, there is not going to be a point where you are perfect enough to handle the anointing. As I say a thousand times, the key is to go to God every morning, for every morning His mercies are new! If I can borrow wisdom from Bishop TD Jakes when he says – "The greatest qualification to be anointed is to feel unqualified." You have the anointing of God flowing through you when God's heart touches another person's heart through your heart. The anointing of God is the Holy Spirit. He flows as a river of love, from the throne of grace, through the hearts of believers, bringing life to all that receive His touch. God anoints people that love Him more than they love their own lives, and that love others as themselves. As we open our hearts to love others God's anointing flows through us. When we close our hearts to others and grieve the Holy Spirit the flow stops and ceases operation. This is why God gives us the anointing so we should not take it lightly and abuse it SELAH…

1 John 3:17 NKJV - *"But whoever has this world's goods, and sees his brother in need, and shuts up his heart from him, how does the love of God abide in him?"*

Proverbs 4:23 NKJV - *"Keep your heart with all diligence, for out of it spring the issues of life."*

The anointing of the Holy Spirit is given through people to demonstrate God's love and power. The term Christ means the "Anointed One". Because Christ is in us the same anointing that He had on earth, he gave to us we also have it as well.

- The anointing is given to preach the Gospel to the poor
- The anointing is given to heal and restore people
- The anointing is given to proclaim freedom to the captives
- The anointing is given to open blind eyes
- The anointing is given to set people free
- The anointing flows in God's timing and proclaims God's timing

Scriptures

Luke 4:18-19 NKJV - *"The Spirit of the LORD is upon Me, because He has anointed Me To preach the Gospel to the poor; He has sent Me to heal the brokenhearted, To proclaim liberty to the captives And recovery of sight to the blind, To set at liberty those who are oppressed; To proclaim the acceptable year of the LORD."*

Prayer

Lord, forgive me for whenever I've taken the anointing lightly. You said in your word that the anointing is the principal thing you need to succeed in any sphere of life, for it is not by might, not by power, but by my spirit says the Lord (Zechariah 4:6). Help me to move by your spirit and be obedient to your word. Lord, help me to seek you first and those things you desire for me. I realize my failures are through disobedience to you. You have given me a great commission and a charge as a leader. Help me to walk this out according to your will. Let me put my selfish ambitious and desires aside so that I can see you will clearly. Thank you, Lord. In Jesus Name I pray, Amen.

OBSERVATION SIX

Owe No Man Nothing

It just shouldn't be this way, but it is. In the body of Christ, yes in the church, you got to be really careful who you accept something from, or who you allow to help you in your time of need. This type of rescue could cause you a lifetime of misery. I've seen leaders that will rescue the people in time of distress, and you think "wow they are doing something noble and honorable and pleasing in the sight of God." Then you applaud their actions only later to find out that they are holding the person that they have helped hostage for the rest of their church life.

Genesis 14: 23 states, that *"I will not take from a thread even to a shoe latchet, and that I will not take anything that is thine, lest thou should you say, I have made Abram rich."* The king of Sodom's made a generous and grateful offer to Abraham, "give me the people and you take the goods". But Abram knew that if he accepted something from this King, it will haunt him for life. That's how it can be sometimes in the in the church when a helping hand is extended to those in need from the wrong person. What is even worse is that we exploit the need in a time of weakness and made giving and receiving a perverted thing in the church. But if somebody is giving to you as the leader, it's all good. I've seen leaders also train the people, teach the people, elevate the people. Then when it's time for the people to leave and move forward according to the will of God, these leaders feel like the people owe them something for what God told them to do or at least that's what they say, "God said". I used to hear, "I've trained them and taught them everything since they been here with me. The last place they were at, nobody taught them nothing and nobody elevated them, they were stuck until they came under my leadership." Yes, they may have been a little bit behind or held back but that's why God release them to you, to right a wrong.

Now let's break this down a little bit further. Do you really think you taught them everything, I mean everything they know, and that their last leadership had no impact in their growth, and you are the only one to take credit for their spiritual journey? So now what does that really mean? If you said you hear from God, and God said or told you to teach the people, elevate the people and train the people, and you hear his voice and you're obedient to His instructions, then why do they owe you anything? What about God? Who owes God? News Flash! We owe GOD everything! Now, take a look in the mirror. Do you really believe that everyone that taught you, trained you, and elevated you, that you owe them your life for all they did for you? If not, then why would you lay this burden on the people that God has entrusted you with. What kind of spirit is that? It is not a good demeanor for the servant of God. As their leaders, the people don't owe us anything, except their cooperation. We are doing what we are supposed to do and what we are called to do. Even if they leave at a time that we deem premature or off schedule, let them go, pray for them, and move forward. I know some leave a bitter taste in your mouth, but we have got to do better in these instances. Please remember, this too shall pass, and God will send you more depending on how you handled the last one. They owe no man anything when it comes to the spiritual things of God. They owe you nothing, if you trust God then that's where your reward will come from. Choose to stop getting in the flesh and remember you deserve nothing back. You were obedient to your calling to equip the saints and you did your job that God required of you. And so, if you really heard from God, and He really told you to do what to do, then do it; but not for personal gain, control, or popularity. SELAH!

What about those who were really active in the Church, giving an abundance of time, talents and treasure to the church above and beyond their tithes and offering. They took care of you and your needs even when they didn't have it to give and even gave you their last, out of love, and you didn't even know that. Now, what do you owe them? How about in the case when pastoral anniversaries and birthdays come around, we act like the people owe us something. And if they don't give us what we want, (i.e. a large sum of money, of course) some leaders get mad and if everybody doesn't give, they get mad. What's that all about? No one owes you anything. They may do it because you taught them honor and let them do because they love you, let them do it because they want to. They shouldn't have to do it out of obligation or fear of retaliation, and even being ostracized. I have seen some leaders get a small gift and ask, "What is this?" or "What I am supposed to do with this?" because they are money hungry. They act out of the greed never knowing the circumstances. That person may have paid their last $20 for the gift and may feel that they rather take their time and buy you something then to just give an envelope with twenty dollars in it! This ungrateful attitude needs to stop. If you say what you do is for the glory of God, then let God get the glory!

Here's a question: If I was locked up in jail and incarcerated for many years and when I got out you took care of me until I got on my feet. Now I'm on my feet and I desire to leave and make a better life for myself. But then you say I can't leave because you were there when I didn't have nothing, now you say I owe you. With that kind of attitude, quite frankly, that person is still in bondage! You are making it hard for them to leave and make their own way. They think they owe you, but if you did it out of the kindness of your heart and acted as God instructed you to do, then guess what that person owes you? Nothing. Release them in your spirit quit holding people hostage!

To the people of God remember, your life is not in the chief cup bearer or the hand of the baker (Genesis 40:1-20). God orders your steps. If it happens, God allows it, and his timing is absolutely perfect. If you're in a situation where you have done something for someone, and you feel they owe you for the favor you bestowed upon them. Some Leaders in this position will treat you good, as long and you are giving them what they need and doing exactly what they say, wrong or right. As long as you're making things happen for them, they're good. You need to rethink this. Stop expecting something in return. Don't worry, God will reward you. And stop looking for that individual to rescue you in your time of trouble. When that individual that you helped doesn't come through for you, you get angry and act like your world will fall apart. Then you lose hope and trust and confidence in others.

This is selfish. Yes, it's selfish and all about self-gratification and being self-absorbed. Just because you rescued a leader at one point or time in the ministry whether it be financial, or serving in any capacity of great need, does not mean that they will remember you when you need to be rescued. It just doesn't work that way.

Some leaders have instant amnesia, so in all you do, do it to the glory of God. That is why it is imperative for us to trust in the Lord and not the strength of Man because they will let you down every time. Man is fickle, but God is faithful. God is the same today tomorrow and forever more He never changes, He changes not, so why not trust in what is sure and guaranteed.

Scriptures

Proverbs 19:17 (ESV) - *"Whoever is generous to the poor lends to the LORD, and he will repay him for his deed."*

Hebrews 13:16 (ESV) - *"Do not neglect to do good and to share what you have, for such sacrifices are pleasing to God."*

Matthew 25:35-45 (NIV) – *"35 For I was hungry and you gave me something to eat, I was thirsty and you gave me something to drink, I was a stranger and you invited me in, 36 I needed clothes and you clothed me, I was sick and you looked after me, I was in prison and you came to visit me.'37 "Then the righteous will answer him, 'Lord, when did we see you hungry and feed you, or thirsty and give you something to drink? 38 When did we see you a stranger and invite* *you in, or needing clothes and clothe you? [39] When did we see you sick or in prison and go to visit you?'[40] "The King will reply, 'Truly I tell you, whatever you did for one of the least of these brothers and sisters of mine, you did for me.'[41] "Then he will say to those on his left, 'Depart from me, you who are cursed, into the eternal fire prepared for the devil and his angels. [42] For I was hungry and you gave me nothing to eat, I was thirsty and you gave me nothing to drink, [43] I was a stranger and you did not invite me in, I needed clothes and you did not clothe me, I was sick and in prison and you did not look after me.' [44]They also will answer, 'Lord, when did we see you hungry or thirsty or a stranger or needing clothes or sick or in prison, and did not help you?' [45] "He will reply, 'truly I tell you, whatever you did not do for one of the least of these; you did not do for me.'*

Prayer

Father, forgive me for trying to take credit and control of what belongs to you. You gave me the voice and the unction of the Holy Spirit to carry out your assignments and speak your word. If I have abused my authority in any way, please wipe away my sins and give me a new perspective and a new heart. Rebuke my selfish ways that I may not go astray. Thank for your love and another chance to get it right. In Jesus name I pray Amen.

OBSERVATION SEVEN

Deliverance is For Everybody…
You Too!

Deliverance is defined as "a rescue from bondage or danger the act of being set free and or emancipated from something. God rescues His people from peril and removes us from being in the midst of trouble or danger from the hand of our enemies and the hand of the wicked. He has given us the great gift of deliverance from our sins, which is available through our Lord and Savior Jesus Christ. Even when we have gone astray or out of His will, He is there for us to repent and get back in His grace and on track again without condemnation. Deliverance is available to you. When we've have attached ourselves to things we shouldn't or even lost our way, we have the assurance that deliverance is still available to us and it's for everyone because we ALL fall short of God glory.

Now, I'm not sure who said that deliverance was only just for the people that are in the church, the carnal and the unsaved only. Whoever said this is dead wrong. Just because we're called to serve and are in a position of leadership and authority doesn't mean we're exempt from needing deliverance. Some Leaders really think that they don't need deliverance because they are leaders and everybody else needs deliverance but them. This is an arrogant attitude and leaders with this kind of mentality are likely the ones who are struggling with the demonic. The sad part about this type of leader is that everybody else can see that but them! We need to learn to recognize when we need personal deliverance. One sign is if you become mean abusive, rude, rebellion, lustful, jealous, and envious. If all of these spirits are hindering you then you may want to take a good look at yourself. And remember that God abides in us and we have the offensive weapons to defeat any demonic attack and overcome evil. The truth is we already have the victory over the enemy and every evil thing. According to 1st John 2:14, we have already overcome the evil one. But we have to accept what and who we are, and recognize when were out of balance and just straight out of order. When things are out of sorts, leaders need to stop saying that nothing is wrong with me and become more self-aware and in touch with yourself. Our main goal as leaders is to keep our focus on the glory of God and His righteousness (Matthews 6:33). This stuff right here is real, the Scripture is clear that demons are real and they interfere in human affairs and they will interfere in our personal lives.

Make the time to get with some other leaders behind closed doors and get delivered from what is oppressing you. If you don't, whatever is on you will spill out onto the sheep. And we've all seen it before. Whatever spirit is on a particular leader, it dwells heavy in the congregation. You can see it, smell it and hear it. You don't want to be the Halloween Church where everybody wears a mask and trick people into thinking they are free and lay hands on the people who think they are getting free. The reason why this is dangerous is that they come back the next Sunday the same way with 7 more demons (Matthew 12:43) all because you ain't free, and you ain't delivered. Yes, this could be a struggle against our fleshly desires but it's time to get free time to get delivered. The devil is a liar! If you are being oppressed in this area, recognize the demons and deal with it. We got souls that are counting on us and we have much kingdom work to do. God makes the way of escape in His perfect will and timing.

 ## Scriptures

James 1:13-15 - *"Let no one say when he is tempted, "I am being tempted by God," for God cannot be tempted with evil, and he himself tempts no one. 14 But each person is tempted when he is lured and enticed by his own desire. 15 Then desire when it has conceived gives birth to sin, and sin..."*

Matthews 12:43 43 - *"When the unclean spirit has gone out of a person, it passes through waterless places seeking rest, but finds none"*

Acts 5:3 -*But Peter said, "Ananias, why has Satan filled your heart to lie to the Holy Spirit and to keep back for yourself part of the proceeds of the land?*

Ephesians 6: 11-13 -*11 "Put on the whole armor of God that you may be able to stand against the schemes of the devil. 12 For we do not wrestle against flesh and blood, but against the rulers, against the authorities, against the cosmic powers over this present darkness, against the spiritual wickedness of this world."*

Ephesians 6:16 – *"In addition to all this, take up the shield of faith, with which you can extinguish all the flaming arrows of the evil one."*

Prayer

Lord I need you, deliver me from every evil thing that's in me. Remove it right now. Burn it out of me anything that is not like you! I have fallen short and have allowed my pride to get in my way. You know everything about me and every hair on my head. Please forgive me for my all ways and my actions that are not pleasing to you. Please heal all whom I have hurt, offended. Restore me as I restore your church to good health. Lord, never let me get far from you. Open my eyes to those things that don't please you, that I may be unaware. Help me to be more accountable. Thank you for the gift of deliverance for all. Thank you that death has no power over us and neither does sin have dominion over me. Please deliver me from me. In Jesus' Name I pray. Amen.

OBSERVATION EIGHT

Abuse: I'm Using My Title to Justify My Actions

Let me be straight forward here. Leaders will use their religious credentials, highly recognized title along with their abusive personalities, their authority and power in the Pastorate office, to justify an un-warranted action. They'll say, "I'm Apostle so and so, or I'm Bishop so and so, or I am Pastor so and so." Why? Because it's allowed, and we allow it, just because they have titles. It seems like when it involves a Pastor, and when I say Pastor, I mean every level of clergy in authority (i.e. Apostle, Bishops, Archbishop and Pastors) or a Leader of the Church, we suddenly apply the no gossip rule, and "don't ask-don't tell" rule. We speak no evil, see no evil, and hear no evil. We are told just to follow the visionary without questioning if whether they are hearing from God or not, no matter how severe the abuse is or who they're abusing.

How do we identify an abusive leader? Well these types of leaders have to have a cheering squad so they hand pick their supporters. They often speak and say that they are proud to say that their, elders, and deacons only disagreed with them only once in 20 something years, and the one in disagreement is no longer at the church; and are proud to say it as if it was an accomplishment for the Church. Now, not knowingly, but what they are really saying is I'm always right. When I heard this in a church setting, immediately my radar went up and says that there is some serious hidden problem in that Church. Pastoral misconduct is real. What ever happened to freedom of speech and truth?

Most church organizations say we are a family, we are one, and we are a church of unity. That's the "keep" word: unity, not the key word. The "keep" word that keeps you in the elusion! Just about every church covenant that I may have read or came across use the term "unity" in it. Another misused word by abusive pastors and leaders. Another trick of the enemy to make it seem that unity means never to disagree with the leader in charge, never, ever, no matter what you think. Your opinion doesn't matter. The scripture in Ephesians 4: 11-16 (NIV) points out the results of unity. And it reads, *So Christ himself gave the apostles, the prophets, the evangelists, the pastors and teachers, to equip his people for works of service, so that the body of Christ may be built up until we all reach unity in the faith and in the knowledge of the Son of God and become mature, attaining to the whole measure of the fullness of Christ.* You see titles in the church are necessary for order and structure, however titles in the carnally led church also enhances power and gives some leaders greater opportunities to hurt or help a person in the church, when it should be used to lead people.

It is evident that unity occurs when we, meaning all of us in the church, become knowledgeable in the faith of God. This knowledge leads to maturity. Unity does not mean saying yes and amen to every whim or word that proceeds out of a leader's mouth. News Flash! Leaders say wrong things because they are human and made of flesh and blood too. Although some leaders have a different mentality, the superhero syndrome, we need to carefully assess the situation, then back up with Scripture what is being proposed, using tact and wisdom, and especially honor to bring it forth. We talk about church maturity, but to tell you the truth maturity may actually involve disagreeing with leadership and to save the church, and save a soul. It's ok to agree to disagree. It might even involve reporting an abusive and unpleasant situation to the authorities or higher up in our leadership chain.

We all have seen this play out in some of our large ministries in the church on television and radio over the years. We were silent and saw and are still seeing the devastation of the outcomes on souls. We have seen leaders who are trusted and revered, abuse members of the congregation and ruined their lives, and the lives of all others who watch this play out on live television, in the news, and in the church. This type of behavior, once out in the news, affects the body of Christ as a whole and it weakens our credibility as Christians and believers. Regardless of whether it didn't happen in your church one incident represent us all. It may not be happening on that level or scale but whether it's happening big or small, it has to be identified and dealt with. Remember, all abuse of titles always starts out small. Abusive leaders like to control people by making them feel worthless. A person that feels worthless or unknowledgeable in the faith can easy be controlled and manipulated to say and do what the leaders wants them to do. This worthless feeling person will also do anything, and everything commanded by this type of leader in order to feel important, and in close relationship to that leader. They want to be in good graces with the leader. These types of leaders will have these people to do all their dirty work for them. They will send them out to ostracize, criticize, and treat another person or member abusively. This means the leader's target to abuse under the directions of another, keeps that leader's hands clean.

When we use are titles in this way, it is unacceptable in the eyes of God. No one is worthless in the sight of God and they should not be abused or be made to feel that way. Our self-worth has already been established at the cross on Calvary. The ultimate price has already been paid. Our redemption was made on the cross. Yes, he thought we were to die for, so we are not worthless people, and we are not entitled to treat others as such. When leaders take titles and proclaim this statement over and over in the pulpit to instill fear: "If you go against a leader, the wrath of God will be upon you." News Flash! The wrath of God is directed for leaders too, if you are disobedient to the will of God. We have got to do better! When we abuse, we separate people from the church and give them feeling of being separated from God, depending upon what level of spiritual maturity.

This excerpt was taken from several reading of how to spot or detect the behavior. This is just something to consider and a time to self-reflect and ask yourself, am I abusive and am I using my title to justify my action? Do you recognized these traits as a leader or in someone you know in leadership?

- I have a huge sense of self-importance and tend to exaggerate my talents and achievements.
- I see myself as someone "special" who can only be understood by other "special" or high-status people.

- I require excessive admiration and feel entitled to special treatment.
- Others are expected to automatically comply with my expectations.
- I take advantage of others to achieve my own goals.
- I lack compassion and am unwilling to identify with the feelings and needs of others.
- I am arrogant and haughty.
- I read demeaning or threatening meanings into innocent remarks.
- I bear grudges and am unforgiving of others I feel have harmed me.
- I am quick to perceive attacks on my character or reputation that are not apparent to others and react angrily or counterattack.
- I am deceitful and seduce others for my own profit or pleasure.
- I am impulsive in my actions and fail to plan think before I act.

Scriptures

1 Peter 5:2-3 King James Version (KJV) -"² *Feed the flock of God which is among you, taking the oversight thereof, not by constraint, but willingly; not for filthy lucre, but of a ready mind;³ Neither as being lords over God's heritage, but being examples to the flock."*

Leviticus 25:43-46 *New International Version (NIV) -"⁴³ Do not rule over them ruthlessly but fear your God."*

Deuteronomy 24:14-15 *New International Version (NIV) -* "¹⁴ *Do not take advantage of a hired worker who is poor and needy, whether that worker is a fellow Israelite or a foreigner residing in one of your towns. ¹⁵ Pay them their wages each day before sunset, because they are poor and are counting on it. Otherwise they may cry to the Lord against you, and you will be guilty of sin."*

Ephesians 6:4- *King James Version (KJV) –* "⁴*And, ye fathers, provoke not your children to wrath: but bring them up in the nurture and admonition of the Lord."*

Prayer

Lord, I am so ashamed as I come before you, you have given me a responsibility to care for your sheep and there are times when I have abused them and abused my authority. Forgive me Lord. It is something in me that needs deliverance and I admit that wholeheartedly today. Deliver me Lord. Fix me from the inside out Lord because no one deserves the pain that I have inflicted. I have been a bad example to the body of Christ I am asking that you turn the situation around let me make it right in your sight, and make amends with those I have done wrong, that they may live a fruitful life and not hold what I done against You or the body of Christ. Help me to start again, according to my original charge given by you and if ever I find myself going back into the bad habits, Holy Ghost arrest me and hold me accountable. I ask this is your most Holy Son name, Amen.

OBSERVATION NINE

I Got Character Flaws

When I say, know your character flaws, what I mean is that you should know the fruit that's rotten on your tree, and what's in improper operation. Sometimes you have to ask yourself a few questions; "What is my love walk like?", "Am I being kind?", "Do I display meekness?", "Is my attitude negative or positive?", "What kind of vibes is my spirit giving off?" Leaders, you should know your flaws and stop trying to act like you're perfect and got it all together. God is perfecting all of us, but you have to know and recognize your own flaws, in order to be all that God has called you to be. Yes, some of us really think we have no character flaws. Yes, really.

It saddens me to see when some leaders get on television being transparent trying to help someone else by confessing their character flaws and Christians trash talk them, mainly because we trying to keep this image that we're so great and we have it all together. But we really need to get it together ourselves. At least they're admitting and know their faults are and chose to improve upon them and build good character. Some leaders really think they got it all together and got something going on. Quit condemning the people, the sheep or others, bashing them for the same stuff you got going on or worst in your own life...it just has yet to be exposed.

I've noticed some leaders can't preach or speak on certain subjects, and that's a sad thing to not have the freedom to preach the whole Bible but just some parts because it will expose your dirt and what you're doing. Why would you continue to be dirty and deprive others of their deliverance? You know exactly what I'm talking about. Some leaders will stay away completely from a certain area of teaching in the Bible...well at least those leaders who have a conscience. Then you have those leaders that will preach on it and speak on it like it's nothing, and you look them the whole time they preaching thinking in your head, "Pastor you know you preaching to yourself right"? But some act like they don't have a clue and they are only preaching to you. Another thing that tickles me on social media where I will see some leaders that will make statement as if they are directing it to someone else and I'm saying to myself "you that person that you trying to talk about". Blind Bartimaeus can see that so why can't you. You mean to tell me you don't know you better than you? Well you might want to ask somebody and believe what you hear. But there is no way you don't know you're talking about yourself unless the devil has really deceived you, got you hoodwinked, or you just in straight denial. Now some stuff we know is elementary. If you check yourself daily and try to walk in a way that's pleasing to God, we know the Holy Spirit has shown you some stuff about you and convicted you on your stuff. For example, now this is just an example, I am not calling you out, but you know the deal. How can you tell the people shacking up in church that this is not the will of God when you got and man or women living in your house with you and you are not married to them? Believe me I've seen some bold preacher in my days, sleeping with people in the congregation on Saturday, and on Sunday preaching about it with an attitude. Talking like the congregation better get it right or God will do such in such to them, but that's you you're talking about. I gather that it's that "do as I say, and not as I do" type of mentality running rampant in the Church. As Leaders we all fall short of the glory, I say that again we all fall short of something, but our goal is to be better, and become an example to the body of Christ. No, I am not condemning or judging, as John 7:24 points out, *"Stop judging by mere appearances, but instead judge correctly."* I'm just judging by what I've encountered through the years. I am not angry at those leaders for that which I saw, but I must admit I felt sorry for them. All that talent, wisdom and knowledge not tapped into, because you limit yourself with sin. We all have to do better. The people should follow us as we follow Christ, not follow us as we stay in sin. Identify your flaws and short coming so you can start helping the sheep and be of help to the others as well. People look up to Pastors and Leaders in the church and believe in them and what comes out of their mouth over the Pulpit. You were there once, but how soon we forget. We have to remember especially the baby saints, and even some seasoned saints that don't spend time in the word, so they fall victim to your nonsense as well. In my reading I've ran across this book called the Chief Feature by Basquiat (1984). He says that the A chief feature is a ***dominant negative attitude*** (meaning that dominate character) — a defensive and potentially destructive pattern of thinking, feeling and acting. We could also call it a constraining factor, or personal stumbling block. We all have at least one. It comes and goes in childhood, solidifies during adolescence, and then surrounds us like a protective shell in adulthood. It seems like a good thing to have at first but, as I will explain, it is based on a false premise and so serves no real purpose. Throughout adulthood it just interferes with our lives by blocking aspects of our true nature and stifling our true character, usually without us even knowing.

Your chief feature is your primary ego defence mechanism and your main stumbling block in life. The article describes how the chief feature comes to have such a stranglehold on our personality. First, though, a general description of the seven possible chief features:

Lolly Daskal: Nobody's perfect, but there are some flaws that are sudden death to good leadership. As you work through your strengths and weaknesses, capabilities and limits, make sure you're steering clear of these dangerous habits:

1. Not setting the example.

When you set yourself apart and fail to "walk your talk," people disconnect. Everything starts with you.

2. Not having a strong vision.

Without a vision you understand and can articulate clearly, you can't impart a sense of purpose and direction to others.

3. Not building people skills.

It's great to be smart, but if you can't be honest and open, if you can't control your emotions or connect with others, you leave a trail of doubt and stress behind you.

4. Not communicating.

If you can't clearly say what you need from people and why you need it, you're never going to get the results you want.

5. Delegating badly or not at all.

If you try to do it all yourself, you create bottlenecks and frustration. And if you delegate carelessly, you create chaos.

6. Forgetting your mistakes.

If you can't open yourself up to learn from your missteps, you're destined to make the same errors again and again.

7. Not fostering emotional intelligence.

If you don't bring empathy, understanding, and camaraderie to your relationships, they will suffer.

8. Ignoring your team's development.

If you fail to invest in your people with opportunities to grow and learn, you're throwing away your greatest resource.

9. Losing your inspiration.

Disconnect from your vision, become complacent, and you'll find yourself with a team that's in it just for the paycheck.

10. Lowering your standards.

If you settle for mediocrity and become willing to maintain the status quo, that's exactly what you'll inspire in others.

11. Resisting change.

If you don't open up to new ideas, you limit innovation and change. If you don't adjust to changing realities, you can't carry your vision and your team into the future.

12. Letting integrity and honesty slide.

Your message, your leadership, your influence is built in part on your flaws. You can try to cover them up with dishonesty and blame, or you can diligently work to improve yourself in everything you do. Whichever one you choose will become your legacy.

Knowing these 12 fatal flaws can help you stop the derailment of your leadership.

 **Scriptures**

Gal 5:22-23 -*"The Fruit of the Holy Spirit is a biblical term that sums up nine attributes of a person or community living in accord with the Holy Spirit according to the Epistle to the Galatians: "But the fruit of the Spirit is love, joy, peace, patience, kindness, goodness, faithfulness, gentleness, and self-control."*

Prayer

My gracious and Heavenly Father you made us so perfect in your image but help me to recognize those character flaws that I have and those that I don't want to face. Help me to stop ignoring the Holy Spirit when convicted and turn from my wicked ways so that I may be healed, able to pour out all that you poured in me without reservation. Release me of the sin I'm in. Wash me with hyssop and make my sin white as snow, create in me a clean heart and search out that hindering spirit that insists on keep me bound. You created me for your purpose so help me fulfill and carry out your perfect plan for my life, in Jesus Mighty name, Amen.

OBSERVATION TEN

Let's Get Back to Holiness

I am going to start out by saying if you are a leader, ask yourself the following questions: Can I preach holiness in the pulpit? Can I handle the heat of conviction when I do preach on holiness? Am I willing to make the change required within myself so that souls may be saved and God's Kingdom can be built? As leaders, this is a must. The Bible says "Without holiness no one will see the Lord" Hebrews 12:14. Holiness is the key to truly understanding and knowing our God. So, do we really want to know God? Are we willing to do what it takes to truly know God? This is why sin is such a serious matter to God. Sin separates us from God. It stands in direct opposition against our heavenly Father, and our testimony becomes corrupted. It quenches and grieves the Holy Spirit. So, what in the world is going on Leaders? Don't you want to see God when all is said and done? This should be your motivation and bottom line. Let's get back to holiness. I know we serve a just God who is faithful to forgive us, but when we try to justify our mess and make excuses for being the way we are, you know God is not pleased. Lay aside the sin that so easily besets you (Hebrews 12:1-2).

You know there are some leaders who still drink, smoke, steal, gamble, fornicate, lie, cheat, steal, and commit adulterous behavior, just to name a few. How are you going to free somebody else when you are not trying or willing to free yourself? I know sin feels too good and has gotten to you, but it is designed to keep you caught up in it and out of the will of God. It's funny, and then again, it's not, but the line I get tired of hearing leaders say is, "I'm not perfect". None of us are. But if you are not trying to perfect yourself and get out of the sin, what is the point of salvation? You have got to make the effort and try to stop with the excuses. God knows that and it's God's grace that keeps us from falling. But listen, it's about choice: either you want to or you don't want to get out of sin and back to holiness. If not, well then, I say this to you, "you don't know God". I've seen some of the same spirits and same attitudes and behaviors for many years on leaders that I've submitted to and sat under who were not trying to change or to get any better. They had gotten comfortable in their mess and nobody ever confronted them. I mean nobody! Even when they heard the complaints or seen the behavior, some even co-signed onto it. They appeared to love being that way and thought it was alright because they were in charge and they were the Leader.

Let's look at the scripture to see what it says about holiness and God's idea of holiness as God presented it to Israel in Leviticus 19. God was instructing them to be distinct from the other nations by giving them specific rules and regulations to govern their lives. Remember that Israel is considered to be God's Chosen nation as God has set them apart from all other people groups. They are His special people and consequently were given standards that God wanted them to live by so the world would know they belonged to Him. Leaders, how will the world know we belong to him if they cannot tell us apart

SAW SOMETHING now I'm SAYING SOMETHING

from the world? When Peter repeats the Lord's words in 1 Peter 1:16, he is talking specifically to believers. As believers, we need to be made distinct and be "set apart" from the world and unto the Lord our God. We need to be living by God's standards, not the world's. Hello! We've got to choose this day who we are going to serve. God isn't calling us to be perfect. But to be distinct from the world. 1 Peter 2:9 describes believers as "a holy nation." This is a biblical fact! We are a special group when we are separated from this world. So, guess what? We need to live out that reality in our daily lives. In 1 Peter 1:13-16, Peter instructs us on how and what to do so we can become this thing called holy. But how? Glad you asked. Holiness only, and I repeat only, results from a right relationship with God by believing in his son Jesus Christ as savior and receiving his gift of eternal life. Remember He is our saving grace. He endured the cross for you and me. If we have not placed our faith in God's Son alone to save us from our sins, then our pursuit of holiness is straight up in vain. All for nothing! I just wanted you to see it in the scriptures firsthand before moving on.

Now somewhere along the way some type of change in the behavior should be noticed or take place but you keep doing the same sinful things over and over again. Remember we serve a just God, don't let your grace run out. Your sin will find you out. We have all seen that happen to many times in the body of Christ. Now get this, you have the audacity and nerve to be disappointed with the people of God because they're not changing, even to the point where you give up on them. Well guess what's happening? You have spread that infected spirit in the fabric on your Church and pour it out upon your people. What's on you is on them too. Aren't

59

your people supposed to resemble you? Well, you know they came from under your leadership and teaching. They are just following the leader. We've all seen it. Some leaders with nasty attitudes, have people in their congregation with nasty attitudes. Maybe they think like you do. Maybe they figured "I can keep on acting that way just as long as I ask for forgiveness" just like you. They say, "Well, Pastor does it". Not so! Keep on carrying on, and God's going to get tired of your mess and God will not be mocked! Time to straighten up and get back to Holiness and the time is now. Let's get it right, get it straight and work on you! This is critical to the body of Christ so let me reiterate:

What is Holiness - the state of being holy. "A life of holiness and total devotion to God". Sanctification of the believer.

An interesting Fact: God never describes Himself as holy until He has delivered the children of Israel from Egypt. When they are camped at the foot of Mt. Sinai for a month of instruction on how they are to live as His holy people, God says for the first time, "You shall be holy, for I the Lord your God am holy" (Leviticus 19:2).

1st John 3:6-10 - *"No one who abides in him keeps on sinning; no one who keeps on sinning has either seen him or known him. Little children, let no one deceive you. Whoever practices righteousness is righteous, as he is righteous. Whoever makes a practice of sinning is of the devil, for the devil has been sinning from the beginning. The reason the Son of God appeared was to destroy the works of the devil. No one born of God makes a practice of sinning, for God's seed abides in him, and he cannot keep on sinning because he has been born of God. By* *this it is evident who the children of God are, and who are the children of the devil: whoever does not practice righteousness is not of God, nor is the one who does not love his brother."*

2 Corinthians 7:1 – *"since we have these promises, beloved, let us cleanse ourselves from every defilement of body and spirit, bringing holiness to completion in the fear of God. And to conclude leaders we must "lovingly" not with brimstone and fire but preach holiness in our pulpits again:*

Hebrews 12:14 - *"Without holiness no one will see the Lord"*

It's not my word but the scriptures. Again, I say ask you, "Do you want to see God?" The prophets of old bear this out as well. These men were sent by God to call the people back to Him...back to holiness: *"And the Lord God of their fathers sent warnings to them by His messengers to get their attention, to convict them, rising up early and sending them, because He had compassion on His people and on His dwelling place. But they mocked the messengers of God, despised His words, and scoffed at His prophets, until the wrath of the Lord arose against His people, till there was no remedy."* **Jeremiah 11:7-11**.

Question to the leaders: Are you willing to do what it takes to truly know God and walk in holiness? **1 Peter 1:13-16** *"therefore, preparing your minds for action, and being sober-minded, set your hope fully on the grace that will be brought to you at the revelation of Jesus Christ. As obedient children, do not be conformed to the passions of your former ignorance."*

Scriptures

On this topic scriptures were placed throughout the reading to get the message across with clarity.

Prayer

My Lord and my Savior and my redeemer, I know that in order to see you, I must be holy. Help me in those areas that I fall short and disappoint you. Help me to stop spreading my infectious ways in the Body of Christ. I know that I am in position to effect and make change. Help me to do so and get it right with you. As David said, when I sin it's against you and you only, Lord. I repent this day of all my sins and iniquities that I have repeatedly done without thought of what you think or require of me. You hold me to a higher standard, and I have not lived up to it, so forgive me Father. Thank you for not exposing me and giving me more time to get it right before you. You are so patient, so loving, and yet a just God. Thank you for covering me. These things I ask in your precious Son Jesus name. Amen.

OBSERVATION ELEVEN

Who's Really Offended, For Real?

Let me start out with this statement: Leaders who get offended and stay offended are dangerous, lethal weapons that carry deadly venom in the church. I've seen some stuff happen in the Churches between a Leader, yes, the one in authority, the head of the congregation and a member and a sheep of the Church! (PAUSE) Jesus! I had to call on Him when I think about some of the stuff I've endured personally and what I have seen others in the body of Christ endure. Here we go…When the initial incident occurs, whatever it is, whatever may occur big or small, everybody is devastated, mad, and everybody is getting in their feelings. I get that this is what some of us do. Sometimes it's a natural reaction until everything settles in and we come to ourselves and we come back to Jesus, and forgiveness takes place. You as the leader *hot as fish grease*, and in some instances rightfully so. But you can't lose sight that you are the Leader and that you set the pace, the temperature, and the tone for the spiritual environment. The Leader should be the first one to get over it, forgive and move forward, especially when it's regarding a sheep in your flock. Sheep do sheep stuff. You know that, and yes it can sting, and hurt you to the core sometimes. Now, I am not saying just dismiss the incident. I know it may take a little time, but your behavior must display differently in public in front of the congregation. Be careful not to bring everybody into this situation and make everybody upset and mad about it. Now, there is a spirit of vengeance in the church. Leaders have to move forward gracefully in public and have a private conversation with Jesus to help us to resolve the stuff that hit us real hard. There is still other sheep to tend to, and there is work to do in the body of Christ and you are charged to do it. We have to learn to move forward for the sake of the Church. Let me say this again. Now, I didn't say you had to forget what happen but at least our outward actions should show, leadership maturity! We need to be the example the leaders under our authority and the ones who are in our care and training. Remember the people are watching you and we don't want them to think that our bad behavior, bad attitude, and hateful disposition is appropriate. I've seen that kind of bad blood spill over in the Church and I'm sure you have too. Yes, you know what I'm talking about... leading while bleeding.

Then, because you are still walking in offense, I've seen you provoke the individual, speak poorly toward them, and find yourself gossiping about them to every other leader that visits the church, using them as a target. But because you in authority, and in charge and this "YOUR CHURCH", (not God's Church but your Church, yes, I said it and you know what I mean by that). You the leader expect the individual not to respond to your constant provoking, criticism, attitude and abuse. Do you know what you're doing? You are provoking the little children? Ephesians 6:4 says, *"Fathers, do not provoke your children to anger by the way you treat them. Rather, bring them up with the discipline and instruction that comes from the Lord."* Are we not spiritual mothers and fathers to them?

We got to do better, in this case, you as the leader will keep accusing the person of being in offense and actually, you are the one still in offense. Usually the sheep know what they did, and the majority of them are sorry, and even sorry they disappointed you. They are going to do everything that can to regain your trust and love from you. They made a mistake and you will use any platform you have to discredit them indirectly and everybody knows who you talking about because you won't let it go, because you keep bringing it up and you are constantly provoking the individual. That's what my statement means in the beginning of this Observation: Leaders who get offended and stay in offense are dangerous, and a lethal weapon that carries deadly venom in the church. For example, the person is already sorry because the hurt or disappointed their pastor and they are making the right moves to reconcile. They are speaking to you and showing you honor and respect, they come up to you hug and love on you. Come on now! They are sheep and they are prone to make mistakes. When they are willing to move on, and you don't and you are steady telling the other leaders under you, they are still walking in offense. Unfortunately, you continue slamming the person over and over in the pulpit with your words. Every leader that visits the church, you have pre-brief them in your office having a discussion on everybody you mad and offended with. You tell them who they are. You give the other leaders permission to call them out and use fake prophesy saying they see a spirit on them. The other leaders call them out and point them out and then every other leader prophesies to them, to make them feel bad, and they are still trying to move. Now who is in offense? Listen, I am not telling you what I heard. I have been in those offices when those intimate, horrible conversations took place and the "set up" occurs. And I've been the one targeted as well. So, I know what I'm talking about. I've seen it too many times... same stuff just different church different leader. Guess what? You are wrong, and the other leader is wrong for co-signing to your mess. They should be helping you get through this praying with you and giving you advice on how to handle this based on their experience, but no. They are not trying to mess up their check. They came to preach to meet your need and get their coins. Get yourself together get out of your feelings and come out of offense, and get in the spirit. You know what they say about feelings, they come and go based on what's going on around you. Stop using your God given authority to justify your offense. And use your God given authority to be an example and walk in love. Luke 7:23 says, "*And blessed is the one who is not offended by me*". Get right and stay in a blessed posture. Withstand the test and get your crown of life for your good deeds which God has promised. Many times, God is trying to get something out of us that He can't use, and in order to take you to the next level, this has to happen. Except God allows, it won't happen. The devil needs permission, and God will allow something to correct a spirit in us as leaders.

When person who committed the offense has repented for any disrespect they have shown you and have moved on to make things right with you and the congregation, why is that is not enough for you. You just can't seem to let things go. You've got to inflict some kind of pain in order for you to feel better. You got to see them beat their head to the ground crying in tears all the time and saying I'm sorry all day long for you to be satisfied, that's not right and you know it! Why is that? As a leader, moving past a situation doesn't take anything from you. It shows good maturity and good a responsible leadership. But in your mind, it shows weakness just because you're exercising meekness and humility. Leaders, meekness is not weakness. It's maturity at its best, so stop tripping and set a good example. You must stay in prayer for that person, and for yourself that you may not cause harm to another. They could end up being one of your greatest leaders. God allows certain things to occur in them. Recognize that this may be in a pruning stage, an incubation, preparation, or learning season. Rebuke, chasten, love and move on. Leaders can be so petty and run something way past its course. Mount up, level up, and do better. People are watching and counting on you to lead with love and integrity.

 **Scriptures**

Proverbs 19:11 - *"Good sense makes one slow to anger, and it is his glory to overlook an offense."*

Ecclesiastes 7:21-22 - *"Do not take to heart all the things that people say, lest you hear your servant cursing you. Your heart knows that many times you yourself have cursed others.*

Proverbs 18:19 – *"A brother offended is more unyielding than a strong city, and quarreling is like the bars of a castle.*

Matthews 18:15-17 – *"If your brother sins against you, go and tell him his fault, between you and him alone. If he listens to you, you have gained your brother. But if he does not listen, take one or two* *others along with you, that every charge may be established by the evidence of two or three witnesses. If he refuses to listen to them, tell it to the church. And if he refuses to listen even to the church, let him be to you as a Gentile and a tax collector."*

Prayer

Heavenly Father, the forgiver of sin and the one who see all things, nothing is hidden from your sight. Forgive me for my immature behavior and dwelling on things that are below and not keeping my mind on the things above. I have not walked in the spirit godliness as I ought to but I have walked in the spirit of offense that is dangerous to me and to those you have given me charge over. Help me in this weak area that I may not dwell in this place again that harms others and doesn't set a good example for the Body of Christ. Search out those insecurities and wounded places in me that still need healing, which are affecting my conduct attitude and behavior. Help me to walk in unconditional love when I am hurting and bring it to you in prayer, casting all my cares to you, leaving it at the altar. Let me make it well with those I have offended. Help me to love on them and teach them your ways and not my own. Thank you for loving me past my mess and allowing me to still serve in this capacity of leadership. In Jesus name Amen.

OBSERVATION TWELVE

"You Know You Can Be Replaced, Right?"

To be replaced is to take the place of, put something back in a previous place or position or restore. How many times out of a leader's anger have you heard this statement? "You know you can be replaced, no love lost here." Let's stop saying that to the people of God. You know they cannot be replaced and you can't be replaced in the eyes of God. God only made one like them just one and even their identical twin is different no matter how much they look alike on the surface; there are many differences to each person.

As far as the ministry assignment is concerned, of course you can get someone to do what they were doing but replacing that particular person God has called to that place; no ma'am, no sir I don't think so. God made one of you, so when he sends you to an assignment, that's your assignment! Let me say that again, that's your assignment! No one was created to do what you do, or to do it how you would do it! He knew exactly what it would take in the assignment, so He slotted you particularly there for that particular one. The lives you will touch in that assignment, no one else will have the same effect on them or make a difference as you do. Someone could say a particular thing to a person and they don't budge. But you can say the same thing to that person and get a totally different outcome and response to motivate them for the purpose just because you are there. That is why when God send someone to a church or under your leadership, your question for Him should be Lord why are they here are they an answer to a prayer? What would God have you for them to do, and let God order their steps and it will be revealed in due time the purpose for which they are sent. The assignment can be two-fold -- for the place they are at, or for a person or a people. God is so amazing while you're on an assignment. You also are in a place that you are someone else's assignment as well, whether it be to teach them or elevate them to the next level. My point is when their assignment is finish, no one can take their place or do what they did like they did, and how they did it, because they were called to it to do it in a special way and therefore lay the foundation and pave the way for the future person's coming after their assignment is up. Think about it! SELAH. Think about what they did for the church and what they brought to the table and what great things they started that now have excelled or exceeded your expectation. An assignment comes with grace and anointing so when they depart their particular grace departs with them!

There is a grace that may stay in the house this allows someone to take over the position they held and take it further sometimes, but not always. This can depend on the spirit in which they departed or perhaps what was going on in the church at that time. No one can take their place, remember and I say again they will not do it the way you did, and they will not get the response or the outcome you have. There are some cases where this part of the ministry could die or lay dormant until God sees fit to send another. I'm not saying that the job won't get accomplished. It will, but the affect will be totally different, and the results of your expectation can prove to be disappointing. No one can take not even your place as a Leader. No two people are alike on this earth so when the saints say it's no big deal someone else will replace them, they may take your place in the position but you cannot be replaced. You are one of a kind an original creation of God the Father. No two persons are alike we have different fingers prints and a different DNA. It's the same with your people, your sheep, stop saying you can be replaced out of bitterness or a rejected place. Accept the decision of difficulty at hand pray for them and wish them well. Let me give you an example. Have you ever been in a conference and the person that led the worship for many years just turns the atmosphere into a taste of heaven? Now this person has moved on to another assignment, the conference goes on at the atmosphere is charged but something seems to be missing and the next person tries to do it like the previous person but it not working and doesn't work. We serve a big God and He is not redundant with his people and His assignments for His people. But the effect is not the same, that's because that grace and that anointing that once was, has left the building and you cannot replace that. The person in your current position will have to do their own thing under the grace that God gives them. And eventually the people will get use to a new way of doing things. But believe me their legacy in that assignment will live on, and years to come you and your people will remember and feel that their presence made a difference, whether you want admit or to acknowledge it or not especially when they were upright and in good standing. Again, I say they cannot be replaced. They can take the position and or title, but they can't take your place.

Scriptures

2nd Timothy 1:1-2 - *(The Message Bible) – "I, Paul, am on special assignment for Christ, carrying out God's plan laid out in the Message of Life by Jesus. I write this to you, Timothy, the son I love so much. All the best from our God and Christ be yours!"*

Ephesians 2:10 – *"For we are his workmanship, created in Christ Jesus for good works, which God prepared beforehand, that we should walk in them."*

Jeremiah 29:11 – *"For I know the plans I have for you," declares the* Lord, *"plans to prosper you and not to harm you, plans to give you hope and a future.*

Prayer

Lord help me to watch my tongue and to stop saying words out of bitterness and anger just because things don't go as I planned, but remind me they are going as you planned. Remind me that I must understand your thoughts are not my thoughts, and your ways are not my ways. Help me to pray for those who leave my church and wish them well and pray that they continue to do the work of Christ. Help me to stop being selfish and let them move on and move in you and with you according to your will. Show me how to give them good counsel and bless them as you would do for me. In Jesus Name, Amen.

OBSERVATION THIRTEEN

Flipping the script

What is flipping the script you may ask? Let's start by defining it. Flip, to turn over or cause to turn over with a sudden sharp movement. Script, handwriting as distinct from print; written characters on a screenplay. And with that defined that's exactly what a lot of us do as leaders and some us of are really good at turning over a word or a phrase, in an instance with a sharp movement that will cut someone with the words out of your mouth. This is done while tipping the conversation to suit them, and by changing the written character of the content in their favor; especially scriptures in the Bible.

Ask yourself are you an expert at this? Truth be told a lot of leaders out there are really good at playing this game. For some leaders, this is their most used tool, and that's why I call it their weapon of mass destruction, because that's how most use it to manipulate and harm others with it! The flipping of God's Word and making scripture fit their desired outcome or situation is just plain ole manipulation and witchcraft. It's like using this as a license to control, confuse and scare the saints into doing what you want them to do. It might sound crazy to some but true that some operate in this devilish realm and God is not pleased. One of the most common scriptures that I heard leaders use and I hear so often is; Psalm 105:15, the word of God say's "touch not my anointed and do my prophets no harm. So what does that really mean? Well here is the context in which it was used, but we take it to a whole other level somewhere else.

David returned Saul's possessions and said, "For the Lord delivered you into my hand but I would not stretch out my hand against the Lord's anointed." (v. 17-24). The Bible makes it clear; to touch the anointed means to bring physical harm and or death. Ok that doesn't mean you can do what you want to a person, or say what you want, or even humiliate them in front of others, by tearing them down and speaking in a rude tone, and then in the same breath say, you can't touch me or you're going to be cursed just as the bible says.

This brief verse contains a powerful warning from the Lord, and He **means** every word of it: **"Touch not mine anointed** and **do** my prophets no harm"** (Psalm 105:15). The real meaning here is woe to any nation or individual who lays a hand on those who are chosen of God. And woe to anyone who **does** harm to his prophets. You are not the only one chosen by God because you have a "title" and are in "authority". You, yourself have got to be careful about who you put your mouth on, and who you treat any kind of way as well. You are not the only one anointed, or the only one called by God. We as leaders don't get to choose who God chooses, and you are not always privy to this information simply by judging those that don't have titles or in a position of authority. Test the spirit by the spirit. I don't how discerning you are, but you need to know who's in your mist. So, the bottom line is you got to treat all of God's people right and respectable. They deserve the same respect that you want and treated them just how you want to be treated.

So please stop the manipulation tactics. You are not the only one anointed and you are not the only prophet in the house. If you really break the scripture down, then it would seem as if you only interpret it for you. So as long as they don't, speak about, touch or kill you, they're good. I bet if you were having a heart attack, chocking or having a stroke and the same ones you persecuted stand there and look at you and say the Bible says touch not my anointed and they stand there and just watch. Then how would you feel? You wouldn't feel because you would probably be dead because no one wanted to touch the anointed one. Now that was food for thought. What about you, are you touching his anointed and doing His prophet harm? SELAH!

 **Scriptures**

Revelation 22:18-19 – *King James Version (KJV)* – *"For I testify unto every man that heareth the words of the prophecy of this book, if any man shall add unto these things, God shall add unto him the plagues that are written in this book: And if any man shall take away from the words of the book of this prophecy, God shall take away his part out of the book of life, and out of the holy city, and from the things which are written in this book."*

Romans 16:17-19 (NKJV) – *"Now I urge you, brethren, note those who cause divisions and offenses, contrary to the doctrine which you learned, and avoid them. For those who are such do not serve our Lord Jesus Christ, but their own belly, and by smooth words and flattering speech deceive the hearts of the simple. For* *your obedience has become known to all. Therefore, I am glad on your behalf; but I want you to be wise in what is good, and simple concerning evil."*

Prayer

Lord, help me to not to manipulate your people, and turn your words to suit me. I am sorry. Please forgive me and help me to treat all of God's people with dignity and respect. Help me to remember you have given me authority to take care of your people not destroy or harm them in any way. You are the one who chose, call, and anoint as you please, not me. Make every crooked place straight in me and cleanse my heart that I may not sin against you. In Your Holy name I pray, Amen.

OBSERVATION FOURTEEN

Why Are You Leaving a Blessed Place?

A blessed place, or a mess place, which one is it? What do we consider a bless place? First let's define blessed which means made holy, consecrated, endowed with define favor and protection, bringing pleasure or relief as a welcome contrast to what one has previously experienced. This definition describes a place where a believer is being in an enviable position for receiving God's provision, favor and love as being and extension of His grace. Since we are made holy through salvation in Christ Jesus, in essence, the most holy and truest form of being blessed is to be made aware of the wretched state of a self-led life, to a repented lifestyle. It means to be sanctified and set apart for holiness and to one day receive the crown of righteousness. When a place of worship is blessed, both those who labor there and those who share the fruit of that labor should feel blessed and experience the blessing. The question that remains is, do we as leaders create an atmosphere where you can feel the spirit of peace, or is it one of tension when you walk in? Is heavy and unpleasant? Well, where do you think that Spirit comes from? One answer to take into consideration is that leaders set the temperature and can be considered the thermometer in Church. You are the head, are you not? Speak now, or forever hold your peace. Now if there is slander back-biting, attitudes, cliques and people not speaking, and speaking ill of one another, is that a blessed place? Right, who are you fooling? Trust me, most leaders, including prophets will walk in the church and know something is wrong. They will feel that spirit in the atmosphere and won't say a word because they just want to collect that paycheck and go home. But isn't that why we invite the prophet to the church to prophecy, dig up and uproot, make aware and warn the saints of what is, and is to come. We must realize that the people in the church and other leaders in the church take on the Leader's personality and spirit, good or bad, but preferably for the good.So, when people in the church discern the corruption or don't feel safe or comfortable, don't get mad when they leave. I say this because Pastors think because they can teach and preach and are very charismatic, and the people are learning, that's good enough. That's what makes the church a bless church? Never mind, that my behavior and the people's behavior, just as long as they are shouting, the music and preaching sound good, and the money is coming in…you think "we are good". Not so! You need to rethink what you are doing and what being blessed really means. Blessed is not wealth or comfort or what I've learned, but rather "being made Holy in the sight of God! Yes, the church is still thriving and blessed through the common grace of God that He extends to all people. However, His grace has an expiration date called Judgment Day. That's all I'm going to say about that, so think really hard when you say this is a blessed place, especially when you got people leaving left and right and leaving for the same reasons. You really need to take a step back when you have your leaders leaving groups at a time, or even one by one, they start to fall off. I say check yourself before you wreck yourself and the church. Think to yourself for real, is God really dwelling there or is the Holy Spirit grieved and the atmosphere reeks of foul play? I suggest you repent and clean your church from the inside out. That means check yourself first and those walking close to you, and then allow God to restore. Don't be the Church of Laodicea found in the bible that we've read in the book of Revelation. We see this clearly in Christ's strong words of warning to the church, and I will end with that.

Scriptures

Revelation 3:14-22 –*[14]"To the angel of the church in Laodicea write: These are the words of the Amen, the faithful and true witness, the ruler of God's creation. [15]I know your deeds, that you are neither cold nor hot. I wish you were either one or the other! [16]So, because you are lukewarm-neither hot nor cold-I am about to spit you out of my mouth. [17]You say, 'I am rich; I have acquired wealth and do not need a thing.' But you do not realize that you are wretched, pitiful, poor, blind and naked. [18]I counsel you to buy from me gold refined in the fire, so you can become rich; and white clothes to wear, so you can cover your shameful nakedness; and salve to put on your eyes, so you can see. [19]Those whom I love I rebuke and discipline. So be earnest and repent. [20]Here I am! I stand at the door and knock. If anyone hears my voice and opens the door, I will come in and eat with that person, and they with me. [21]To the one who is victorious, I will give the right to sit with me on my throne, just as I was victorious and sat down with my Father on his throne. [22]Whoever has ears, let them hear what the Spirit says to the churches."*

1 Thessalonians 4:10-12 – *"We urge you, brothers [and sisters], to progress even more, and to aspire to live a tranquil life, to mind your own affairs, and to work with your [own] hands, as we instructed you, that you may conduct yourselves properly toward outsiders and not depend on anyone.*

Prayer

Lord, have mercy upon me. I have allowed sin in the camp that has killed the fruit of the vine. Father, forgive me and bring the church back to righteousness so that your spirit may dwell there gain. Anything that's not like you, please remove it from your church. Anything within us that is not like you, chasten, rebuke, and remove it that we may freely call this a blessed place with pure heart. There are souls at stake. Let those who come into the house recognize and feel your Holy Spirit. Thank you, Lord. Help us, to get it right. In Jesus name we pray Amen.

OBSERVATION FIFTEEN

I Got Power on Social Media

Why do we hide behind social Media? We trash talk and write things on Facebook, Instagram and Twitter that sound really good and very convincing to those who don't know you. We talk the talk, but we don't walk the walk. The world sees the talk, but the people who really know you see the walk. Those leaders are just writing stuff to be writing stuff and don't really believe what they are writing. For example, they quote "love thou neighbor as thyself" but are constantly throwing shade at the people and leaders in their own house. They are mad and holding grudges while being very unforgiving, but on social media you say, "love one another". This leader stays mad for months because somebody under their authority did something they didn't like, or they have left the church. And then when people leave the church, the leader acts like they killed somebody and must be punished by lethal injection or even given the death penalty. Then they slander their name using rude and aggressive comments that blatantly states the obvious. Anybody with any inkling of discernment can see through your anger and aggression and realize there is some drama going on in that church. It's easy to detect all your comments on social media are hateful, bitter and abusive.

This is not the way to behave as a leader no matter what. Leaders are to be the bigger person here and not hang out all the dirty laundry. How soon we forget. You forgot the time when you left a church. And for some who didn't leave a church in good standing because the level and intensity of the situation and was only doing what God told them to do, which is RUN! Anyway, you did what God commanded you to do and what was in your heart based upon the circumstances presented. As a Leader, we are to pray for the wisdom of God's timing and pray that the decision made to leave the church was clear instructions from God, and then we wish them well, pray over them, and leave it alone. Besides, who are we to question it? I know some people do leave prematurely because they mad about something or they didn't get their way, etc. But I get it! We can't account for their behavior, but we can surely account for ours. Listen, putting slanderous posts on every platform of social media you can is unacceptable. We have got to let it go.

Now, what if they did make a mistake and left too soon or out of anger. And at one point you realized they shouldn't have left, or they left and now want to come back. Your behavior and the way you conducted yourself doesn't give them any room to return or reconcile with the church, causing even more souls to turn away. We have to put ourselves in other people's shoes and think how we would feel if this was done to us. It's sad but leaders need to get delivered from this because hurt leaders, hurt people. Please remember that the lens you are looking through is bigger than you. This is a soul and a sheep that has gone astray. You quote scriptures about forgiveness and you even preach on forgiveness, but you can't forgive. What's wrong with that picture? We must be a better example to the body of Christ than that. What I always tell leaders is keep provoking the sheep or other leaders under your leadership if you want to, but everybody is not scared of your title or even care if you in authority. All that goes out the window and all bets are off when you act foolishly to some saints. Remember that God is still working on folks and they not scared of you! Do you realize you can cause that same aggression to come back on you or even worse? Need I say more? You can hide behind social media, but when someone confronts you face to face with anger and aggression you don't know what they are capable of doing. You don't want to provoke the children or the spiritual sons and daughters or even the wayward stepchild. Let's be wise as a serpent and innocent like a dove. It's already hard out in this cruel world, so let's not be contributors to the problem and do better and love them unconditionally, despite what they do.

Scriptures

Ephesians 6:4 - *"Fathers, do not provoke your children to anger by the way you treat them. Rather, bring them up with the discipline and instruction that comes from the Lord."*

Gal 5: 25-26 - *"If we live by the Spirit, let us also walk by the Spirit. Let us not become conceited, provoking one another, envying one another"*

Hebrews 10:24 - *"and let us consider how to stir up one another to love and good works."*

Prayer

My Lord, what have I done? Please forgive me for using a platform that can save lives to destroy them. I have abused my authority and given up my good voice to harm your people. More is expected of me. Help me to exercise more self-control and be slow to take offense and quick to hear your voice when I'm not pleased with the action of others. Forgive me for bringing shame to the church and to the body of Christ. The Church belongs to you not us. Just because we are in authority; we are merely stewards over it and at times have abused our authority. Please forgive me. I repent of my sins, help me to love unconditionally like you and deliver me from all unrighteousness and heal those wounded places in me. In Jesus Name I pray. Amen.

OBSERVATION SIXTEEN

My Bible say's Honor "Me"

"My Bible say's honor me and that's what I want honor. I want honor and respect, because I'm in charge and in authority." Believe it or not, I've heard this come out of the mouth of some leaders. If you are a leader in authority ask yourself, "am I'm giving honor and respect back to others under my authority?" We want all the honor and respect, but we fail to give it back to others who are under our leadership. Now, what is that really all about? 1st Timothy 5:17 (EIV) says, *"Let the elders who rule well be considered worthy of double honor, especially those who labor in preaching and teaching."*

This is one of my favorite scriptures and I believe wholeheartedly that it should be according to the scripture. I always revered my leaders according to the scripture and loved on them above and beyond to show them my appreciation for their labor. My observation of almost 20 plus years in ministry has been that some leaders are so disrespectful, abusive, and downright mean in their actions and harsh with their tongues.

We know when a leader is like that there's more to it than meets the eye. (i.e. - it could be insecurities, pride, needing deliverance, unfaithfulness, their lack of relationship with

God, or sin.) Some may have never been in charge and just don't know how to lead and are leading pre-maturely. It could be a number of things, but they need to be addressed. Now let's put the shoe on the other foot. Let someone disrespect you and treat you the way you treated them, and you would think the world has come to an end. Your flesh rises up and all of the hell in you breaks loose. Remember this: I'm an eyewitness to it. You basically want to execute that person by a firing squad if you could. You want to get rid of them fast with swift justice.

I think you got where I'm coming from, now let's switch gears. Explain to me, why you require the extra, extra, extra over the top honor? I know the Bible say's give double honor, I get that, but you want triple and quadruple honor. What's going on with you? Let the saints give that extra honor to God, who is way more worth of it. I went to a Church in my city where I live and it was pretty nice size church. You could consider this a mega church, and this was one of my first observations as I attended worship there. The praise and worship was good, but I felt that they could have given God a little bit more of themselves, in my opinion. There was a big choir and lots of musicians. It could have been me because I stay thirsty for His presence, but I just felt they wasn't giving God their full worship. The atmosphere felt a little restrained and programmed. I say this because I was going all in just thinking about the goodness of Jesus and I felt a little uncomfortable and out of place like I was doing too much for them. Maybe it was the side eyes I was getting but I just kept doing what I do. Now as soon as the worship was over, (as far as I was concerned, it could have keep going for a while longer but like I mentioned it felt programmed, like now "let's go", and now "let's stop") the worship leaders said to the congregation and said put your hands together for our Pastors, Bishop Peach-head and Pastor Watermelon, not Jesus, but the Pastors. As they began to honor their Pastors, which I thought was great, until the people started losing their minds they were shouting, dancing, screaming, jumping up and down, running in the aisles and really carrying on. You could imagine what this looked like to me. When they mentioned the name of their Pastor, I honored them with the clapping of my hands and asked God to bless them, but again I felt out of place, like I was doing something wrong. They were over the top with this honor, if there is such a thing. Then I said to myself, maybe it's just me but something is wrong with this picture, I thought to myself they have made their Pastors their God. Where did they get that from? Okay I said to myself again (under my breath of course because I wasn't trying to get thrown out the church), maybe it's just me. As service continues, I believe after announcements or something, someone else came up and said come on let's give God some honor, glory and praise. Then the person on the microphone begin to exalt God but the responses were minimum. Nobody was running, break dancing or doing flips like that stuff I saw earlier. That's when I thought to myself, "I don't believe this somebody has hoodwinked them. They are honoring the Pastors more than they are honoring God. Oh my God!" The second thought I had that came to my mind was this is straight up cult activity in this house. I wondered what in the world they got going on here? It wasn't a bad church, and they weren't bad people...so what was happening here? What was it that was being required of the people by their Leaders because this behavior flooded the atmosphere, so it had to come from the top! I also noticed that if you didn't get in on the flips and the cartwheels when they were honoring the Pastors, they gave you the side eye and looked at you like you were crazy, like *"you better get with the program"*. And if you did too much shouting for Jesus and started speaking in tongues, they basically without saying it, wanted you out of the church because, according to them, you weren't a good fit. There was no doubt that I was being watched and it was clear that they had they eyes on you.

Let's go back to this scripture again. The bible clearly states give honor to your leader. 1st Timothy 5:17 reads, *"let the elders that rule well be counted worthy of double honor, especially they who labor in the word and doctrine."* But there is a line that leaders distinctively know that they should not crossed, because they are not greater than God. And, we are not greater than our God and we as leaders should make clear to the people that our God is greater and worthy of the honor and praise and there's nobody greater than Him. If you, as the leader are allowing that behavior, this is absolutely unacceptable. The sad thing is that it was so evident to anyone that was new or visiting the church. It was so obvious and noticeable. And over the years after God released me to go do greater works, when asked if I still go to that church, that would be the first thing they mentioned, even for those who just visited a few times in search of a church home. The sad thing is that you as a leader get mad when they mention your name and no flips or cartwheels are done, you get mad and call it disrespect. In other words, some people were just following suit because they think that is what is required by the leader. Again, it felt cultish. I believe it is still an earned privilege to be honored with sincerity from the heart and doing it because the word of God said it...and it comes from the depths of your heart to do in love for your leader. That's the way I would want to be honored, and so should you as a leader -- not because they have to, or have to act a certain way to fit in, but because they mean it from their heart. You should only want to be honored because they believe in the God in you, and they are sincere about the love they have in their hearts for you. How are you really being honored? Is it just a routine or do the people really love and honor you? Or are they just honoring your position and following the scripture. I suggest you take inventory. Make an observation and just think about it. SELAH

 **Scriptures**

Ephesians 6:9 - *"And masters, do the same things to them, and give up threatening, knowing that both their Master and yours is in heaven, and there is no partiality with Him."*

Leviticus 25:43 - *"You shall not rule over him with severity, but are to revere your God."*

Deuteronomy 24:14 - *"Thou shalt not oppress an hired servant that is poor and needy, whether he be of thy brethren, or of thy strangers that are in thy land within thy gates:"*

Prayer

Father, in the matchless and mighty name of Jesus I repent of my sins. You are the Almighty God and you share your glory with no man. When I made myself a god for others to worship, I went against all you stand for, forgive me Lord and give me a spirit of humility. Holy Spirit, when I get off course, haughty and prideful. Convict me and correct me when I get wayward in my ways. Lord, help me to lead the people out of error. Let me decrease that you may increase as Lord over my over my life. You are the Lord God and there is no other. In Jesus name I pray Amen!

OBSERVATION SEVENTEEN

Nice but Nasty, with a "Get Back" Spirit

A nice but nasty person is someone or should I say a person who pretends to be *nice* but will talk about you in your face and you not even notice it until they walk away, or you later recall the conversation that took place. They can be kind, soft spoken and say kind words to you one moment, but at the same time their behavior is devious. Behind your back they are plotting your demise or speaking ill of you to others.

Have you ever done something to somebody you didn't mean, and you apologize for what you've done and even show remorse but yet still they insist on getting even? They feel they have to even the score by wanting you to pay for that mistake, whether big or small. Well this is what it's like for some leaders who won't be satisfied until that person is totally humiliated. Now here is where the "get back" spirit enters. To get back at someone is to retaliate, usually through a counterattack. It's a need to do something to hurt or upset someone after they have hurt or upset you. You can do something to them, and they didn't like it, again it could be big or small or even irrelevant, but they want to always have the upper hand. It's that "I'm in control" or "I'm the boss" type of spirit. Like I mentioned before you could have said I'm sorry I was wrong, and it won't happen again and even ask for forgiveness. They will pretend and have you under the pretense that they have forgiven you and have moves on, but not so. Many of us have met leaders like this or are like this. I have experienced this firsthand. After the incident, you speak and they will halfway speak, and halfway smile, and give you the side eye as if to say I got my eyes on you and it isn't over. But when they are in the presence of someone that has influence or superior to their title, they are nice in their tone, but their actions prove otherwise because they do nasty stuff and then try to justify it as necessary.

Some leaders will go as far as when you do something wrong, they will act like it's no big deal and even say we all make mistakes, its part of your spiritual growth, as if they mean it. Then they say they have forgiven the incident but at the same time they are scheming to get you back, and they will believe me, do it by any means necessary. The individuals that experience this from a leader will be caught off guard because they trust the leader. They trust that what you say is what you mean, and they can take from this experience the lesson learned and move on in ministry. They continue to be nice to you around other people but have a real nasty spirit around you when you alone or no one is around that has any influence. This is a dangerous spirit. This spirit will lie on you, deceive you, it harbors unforgiveness. It's vindictive, controlling, and this spirit back bites too. It recruits and gathers other sheep and leaders to join their team against you. It's like they get in a huddle and say, "team we got to get him/her". These types of leaders want you around as long as you don't shine brighter than them and don't disagree with their foul behavior. Once you realize that what they are doing isn't God, and they know you figured it out, you become the enemy.

They will give you things, feed you, and let you come into their presence sometimes for special occasion to fellowship with other influential people because these other people may speak highly of you and your servitude, that's their nice side. The nasty side comes out if they see you getting any kind of attention and highly spoken of as being a good influence on others as a well-respected a leader in your own right. And don't you dare have an opinion, even if they asked the group what they think…and don't dare disagree with them. Oh no, that's when the "get back spirit" comes alive and they won't get you one on one, they will wait until they get an audience of a crowd of other leaders or other sheep. They clown you and embarrass you until their flesh gets satisfaction. It could go on for months and maybe even years, but the flesh is never completely satisfied. You know as leaders, we do too much with that and this is not the Spirit of God. We need to cut this out and get in prayer and bring that flesh under subjection, God has too much work to be done in the body of Christ.

Scriptures

Proverbs 20:22 – *"Do not say, "I will repay evil"; wait for the Lord, and he will deliver you"*

Romans 12:19 – *"Beloved, never avenge yourselves, but leave it to the wrath of God, for it is written, "Vengeance is mine, I will repay, says the Lord."*

Proverbs 24:29 – *"Do not say, "I will do to him as he has done to me; I will pay the man back for what he has done."*

Romans 12:17-21 – *"Repay no one evil for evil, but give thought to do what is honorable in the sight of all. If possible, so far as it depends on you, live peaceably with all. Beloved, never avenge yourselves, but leave it to the wrath of God, for it is written, "Vengeance is mine, I will repay, says the Lord." To the contrary, "if your enemy is hungry, feed him; if he is thirsty, give him something to drink; for by so doing you will heap burning coals on his head." Do not be overcome by evil, but overcome evil with good*

Ephesians 4:26 - *"BE ANGRY, AND yet DO NOT SIN; do not let the sun go down on your anger."*

Ephesians 4:29 - *"Let no unwholesome word proceed from your mouth, but only such a word as is good for edification according to the need of the moment, so that it will give grace to those who hear."*

Matthew 5:22 - *"But I say to you that everyone who is angry with his brother shall be guilty before the court; and whoever says to his brother, 'You good-for-nothing,' shall be guilty before the supreme* court; and whoever says, 'You fool,' shall be guilty enough to go into the fiery hell."

Ephesians 4:31 - "Let all bitterness and wrath and anger and clamor and slander be put away from you, along with all malice"

James 1:19 - "This you know, my beloved brethren. But everyone must be quick to hear, slow to speak and slow to anger;"

Prayer

Ruler, Savior, Redeemer, please crucify my flesh and take over this sinful body, mind and spirit. Cast out anything that's not like you. Forgive me for my behavior and allowing the enemy and the inner me to do ungodly things against others who trusted me to be a good example. Remind me every day to bring my flesh under subjection, that I may be a blessing and not a curse to your people in whom you entrusted to my care. In Jesus Name I pray, Amen.

OBSERVATION EIGHTEEN

We Say, "Greater Works Shall You Do"

W e casually roll these words off of our tongues a scripture from the word of God and say to those under our leadership, "greater works shall you do". Yes, greater works, just as long as the work you do is not greater than my works and all eyes are still focused on me and my gifts. This is just crazy to me and even comical at times to watch, but we have leaders in the church that quote the scripture like they mean it until challenged with the reality of the scripture coming to past. When we say it, it sounds good, but do they really mean it?

John 14:12 says, *"Verily, verily, I say unto you, He that believeth on me, the works that I do shall he do also; and greater works than these shall he do; because I go unto my Father."* This scripture is for all of us, and God is no respecter of persons. His word is not limited to the shepherd of the house this is for all that believes in Him. So what happens when those under your authority begin to do the greater works? Don't be dismayed. The works they are going to do should be unto God, not unto you. You will give a person on your leadership team greater responsibility to take the load off of you and make your plate lighter with an intricate series of training to take them to the next level. You even inform the congregation what you are making this leader responsible for, and you read the laundry list of things you would have them to do. Then you close by saying, I need you to take these things to this leader to resolve before you bring them to me. I have a lot on my plate and in this season, I'm focusing on such and such. Now things are going well, and this leader is making it happen, training other leaders, taking care of your affairs as directed and doing really well. Everybody loves them. They are humble compassionate and just got the church thriving and moving in a good direction following your lead. Now that the people are coming to this leader with everything you told them to, then all of a sudden you start feeling some kind of way about the leader you selected. You begin a power struggle, coming totally out of the spirit. All the attention is not on you now and it's on that leader you are training to stand in your shoes. This person is being groomed to potentially take your place in your absence someday as you go out and build churches and go speak to nations. Now that they are thriving doing really well, they are being respected, but oh, oh… here we go… you allow the enemy to creep in, in the form of a jealous spirit. And when that jealous spirit is in full effect, it's a monster that will kill your relationships and potentially kill a ministry. Now that things are shifting and they are doing greater works and the people have a love for that leader, this does not take anything away from you, your position, or your leadership. But because you are not self-aware of your behavior and attitude and what the enemy is doing, you start up with your mess in the pulpit, the sacred altar, saying stuff like, "Some of ya'll trying to be me, but don't forget, I'm in charge, there is only one head in this house, and leadership with two heads is a monster. Instead of addressing the issue, you go about things the wrong way and in an immature fashion. You hold meetings and say I think someone of you leaders are being deceitful, you carry on and on and won't let it go, until it becomes obvious you are talking about that particular leader. Now instead of calling the leader in one on one with your concerns, you cause a rift in leadership and in the church, then there is bitterness and rivalry and leaders taking sides and all kinds of mess began to surface.

Stop quoting scripture and don't mean what you say! Say what you mean and mean what you say! Again, if you're going to quote the scripture mean it. When your leaders do greater works, remember this is a direct reflection of your good training, guidance, and equipping. It is also the result of the leadership of those who have come before you whom they have served and equipped in their life. There is nothing to be jealous of, and everything to proud of. Let them grow. Let them thrive. Correct and chasten them when needed but don't bring that flesh and jealous spirit in your house or breed the spirit of envy over your altar and in your house. Let's do better, so they can do better.

Scriptures

James 3:14-16 - *"But if you have bitter jealousy and selfish ambition in your hearts, do not boast and be false to the truth. This is not the wisdom that comes down from above, but is earthly, unspiritual, and demonic. For where jealousy and selfish ambition exist, there will be disorder and every vile practice."*

Proverbs 27:4 - *"Anger is cruel and fury overwhelming, but who can stand before jealousy?"*

Prayer

Father, you have entrusted me with vessels to teach, train and equip. You said that all in Christ will do greater works and that just doesn't just apply to me, but to all believers. Forgive me for my selfish ways and for letting the enemy take over something that was meant to be pure. Create in me a clean heart that I may do what you called me to do for your people and not stand in the way of what you're doing in their lives. Heal the spirit of jealousy because it is a sickness that can spread and kill the entire body of Christ. Thank you for deliverance and healing in Jesus Name I pray. Amen.

OBSERVATION NINETEEN

I'm a Pulpit Bully

Yes, there is a definition for a bully pulpit described in Wikipedia, but in the church, it's a pulpit bully. Same meaning just reversed in the way it's presented. Are you what we consider to be a pulpit bully picking on the people just because you can, and just because you're in authority and have a platform to do so? Is that you, Shepherd and servant of the Most High God?

Let's break this down so you're clear on identifying yourself, if this is you. A bully pulpit is provided a conspicuous position that provides an opportunity to speak out and be listened to. This term was coined by United States President Theodore Roosevelt, who referred to his office as a "bully pulpit", by which he meant a terrific platform from which to advocate an agenda. Yes, your agenda!

The Urban dictionary says it is someone who harasses or intimidates. Sound familiar? It should, because we see it all the time and we allow it to! As leaders we justify it by constantly saying nobody wants to be rebuked or take correction. And if it hit a nerve, then that might be you. I have seen many leaders guilty of this behavior.

Help me out with this question leader: how do you talk to a leader who always, or should I say consistently uses the pulpit to put down people or break their spirit? Or you use the pulpit to put down other ministries, and you always seem to live in a constant state of rebuking and correcting the church instead of lifting up God's church.

In so many words, let me make this plain, "How do you deal with a Pulpit bully?"

This is for real leaders and you know what I'm talking about. First of all, bullies exist in all walks of life: in the streets, schools, workplace, sororities, fraternities, organized groups, and organizations, and even at home. We see it just about everywhere and lately we hear about people being bullied all the time. But how did we let this creep over into the church, that sacred place where people come to get a relief from the cares of the world. Now, it went from the streets to the church and right into the leadership and straight to the pulpit. All of us have had the experience in life of probably being bullied or then again you may have been the bully. I'm sure if I ask you about a time in your life when you were bullied, you would definitely reflect and have a story to tell.

We don't easily forget these horrible experiences because they can be life changing. Just think about the children in schools that were bullied to the point of suicide. It's an unfortunate rite of passage to the young people, especially during those adolescent years. Some get over it and some never survive it, which is a sad state for the school system. So why would we bring this in the Church that is supposed to be a place where you can go get help, get fed, get nourished, get restored, and replenished. The church is supposed to be a place of refuge to retreat from the cares of this cruel world even if it's only but for a moment. It's a place to bring those trials that we are dealing with as well as a place to grow from stagnation. It's the place to spend time as a family in the Body of Christ and a place of love and hope where you can learn about our Lord and Savior Jesus Christ. You see what I'm getting at, so I say again why do some leaders bring bullying into the church? This can't be taken lightly. I have seen Pulpit bullying ruin people lives, derail destiny, kill a spirit, and people's journey toward God. I've seen some just plain give up on the church.

We as Leaders have to remember everybody don't have our strength or mind, just because they are in the church every Sunday. Now if that was so, there would not be all the suicides that are committed. It would have never happened because we all are the same but that's not true. Not everyone can take that kind of pressure and humiliation. Some of us may not have a clue to how or what it means to be bullied by a leader/pastor, but I my bet is the majority of us do. Remember, I'm speaking from experience.

You see the worse place to bully someone is over the pulpit. It's the worse place for the victim, but the ideal place for the bully. I say this because that's a place of authority, the place where all attention is given to that only voice speaking and has a platform that says "I'm in charge and I can say what I want. I command the attention of the room and I can do whatever I want." I've seen all the sneaky and tricky ways some leaders approach your target. You see leaders can be very clever and cunning in attack. Let me give you an example, I bet your leader has never stopped you in the church hall or right before or after a service, and jacked you up by the collar like real bullies or taunted you in front of other church going saints. Nor have they thrown you against the wall and demand something or ask something of you picked at you via social media. No, that that's not likely, because they have a reputation and an image to protect. But if I had the choice, I'd rather you man up or women up, and do me this way than to get in a sacred space and tarnish God's pulpit with your gangster spirit. I have seen some leaders preach an entire sermon criticizing, ostracizing, slandering the people of God and anybody under the sound of their voice that had a disagreement with them. The crazy thing is they may not even be talking to you or about you, but you feel some kind of way because of the delivery of their words and spirit behind it. They have shouted brimstones and shot fiery darts, slam their hands and hit the pulpit, shook their fist like a gangster and disfigured their face to get their point across to whosoever will. The first time I saw it, and numerous times since, I said that's just crazy and I could not believe what I was hearing. I almost forgot I was in church until they said it's offering time. But little did I know years later, I would have the privilege of experiencing that kind of hatred from the pulpit not once but twice. Yes, I said the privilege because God showed me something about leaders and the Body of Christ. It taught me something. It showed me church reality. I was sleeping in la-la land, but this woke me up from a sleep and an illusion of church and religion. So, I count it all joy. Thou He slay me yet will I trust Him. What I saw and what I experienced was not sacred and not what I believe was God. It appeared to be that was demonic. Leaders, the pulpit is not the place or time to air your anger lose control and abuse your power. Get help and get some deliverance.

This is the kind of cold-hearted, bullish ways, which are so un-pastoral. This is selfish immature behavior of a leader that does it this way because they don't want to hear nothing nobody has to say. They have no interest in hearing you and don't want your input, or want you to express your freedom of speech. The majority of people have respect for a person that mounts the pulpit so not too many people are going to say anything while that leader is ratting and raving over the pulpit. They may walk out, because I have walked out, but not too many are going to say anything. A lot of time it catches us off guard and by surprise and most of the time it's so surreal you can't believe the words that are coming out of their mouth. You can't believe that it happening so you just stay frozen to your seats listening and making sounds like "what the hell" under your breath. This is a self- righteous person that thinks just because they are the leader of the church it's their right and prerogative to do what they do and it's alright to do this type of stuff they do…wrong answer.

So what Leaders, if somebody provoked you and criticized you, gossiped about you, lied on you, broke your heart, or did something that didn't agree with. You're supposed to be built for this. God conditioned you for this. You are called to this. You are anointed for this. And they did it to Jesus who paid a debt He did not owe -- the ultimate price which our suffering can't compare. You know that's what sheep do and that's what people do in and outside of the church. When you cut up like this, it shows just where you are in your walk with Christ. Stop exposing yourself and your walk and relationship with Christ. You may shout, preach and teach the house down but my concern is where do you stand with God? Don't just talk the talk, walk the walk. Have you ever thought I am just talking to the leaders? If you are the bully, what do you think God thinks of your behavior? Is He pleased or do you even care? It is these kinds of actions that cause the pulpit to no longer be sacred. The Holy Ghost will depart an atmosphere is tainted and you have blood on your hands. Is it really worth it? Food for thought, open your eyes leaders, if it leads to suicide in the schools what makes you think it can't lead to the same in the church? This is serious and we need to address it as such. We just don't know where people are in their walk and what's going on in their lives. Don't be the one to cause a soul to lose the race. This is personal for me because I have had to talk a few souls off the ledge at the brink of suicide. Fortunately for the believers we have a choice of churches and we have free will to move about and relocate as we please. I think that's the only thing that has saved the body from a trend of tragedy in the church. Thank God for free will! SELAH! This is not everybody, and for those who are doing the right thing and doing it the right way scripture says you're blessed. Matthew 5:10 says that God blesses those who are persecuted for doing right, for the Kingdom of Heaven is theirs. Matthew 5:11 says God blesses you when people mock you and persecute you and lie about you and say all sorts of evil things against you because you are my followers. 2 Corinthians 12:10 says "For the sake of Christ, then, I am content with weaknesses, insults, hardships, persecutions, and calamities. For when I am weak, then I am strong." Here are a few quotes to think about:

"Pulling someone down will never help you reach the top." Abhishek Tiwari

"Be sure to taste your words before you spit them out."

"A negative mind will never give you a positive life."

"Blowing out someone else's candle won't make yours shine brighter."

Christians should always look to God for guidance for any situation that we're in. God loves you. Every obstacle in life is for a reason. It is building you up. Be strong, God will help you. Luke 6:35 says to love your enemies! Do well to them. Lend to them without expecting to be repaid. Then your reward from heaven will be very great, and you will truly be acting as children of the Most High, for he is kind to those who are unthankful and wicked.

Scripture Message to the Bullies

1. *Matthew 7:2 for with the judgment you pronounce you will be judged, and with the measure you use it will be measured to you.*

2. *Matthew 7:12 so whatever you wish that others would do to you, do also to them, for this is the Law and the Prophets.*

3. *Isaiah 29:20 for the ruthless shall come to nothing and the scoffer cease, and all who watch to do evil shall be cut off.*

4. *Matthew 5:22 But I say, if you are even angry with someone, you are subject to judgment! If you call someone an idiot, you are in danger of being brought before the court. And if you curse someone, you are in danger of the fires of hell.*

5. *Philippians 2:3 Do nothing from rivalry or conceit, but in humility count others more significant than yourselves.*

Scriptures

1 John 2:9 – *"whoever says he is in the light and hates his brother is still in darkness."*

James 2:8 – *"if you really keep the royal law found in Scripture, 'Love your neighbor as yourself,' you are doing right."*

Matthew 19:19 – *"honor your father and mother, and love your neighbor as yourself."*

Leviticus 19:18 – *"you shall not take vengeance or bear a grudge against the sons of your own people, but you shall love your neighbor as yourself: I am the Lord."*

2 Timothy 1:7 – *"For God gave us a spirit not of fear but of power and love and self-control."*

Prayer

Lord help me. I repent of my sins. When I sin, it's against you and you only. Deliver me from me. Forgive me for all of my wrong deeds, (begin to name them). Forgive me for all the lives I've destroyed and all the souls I have hindered from experiencing you in such a pure way. Restore and recover what I've done, help me to complete and utterly turn from my wicked ways. Forgive me for bringing shame and embarrassment to the body of Christ. Thank you for covering my sins with your love, help me to love like you love and keep your commandments. In Jesus Name I pray, Amen.

OBSERVATION TWENTY

I'm Greedy, I'm Controlling, and I'm Prideful

Greed - intense and selfish desire for something, especially wealth, power.

Control - the power to influence or direct people's behavior or the course of events.

Pride - feeling or deep pleasure or satisfaction derived from one's own achievements.

W hen you're dealing with a leader that has these three spirits, look out and run for your life because this is a lethal destructive combination. These behaviors can totally disqualify us and interrupt our obligation and duties as leaders. As leaders again I say we need to be self- aware of how we really are and how we perceive ourselves to be. We need to come clean and own our stuff and admit our weaknesses and faults. The bible says in James 5:16 to confess *your* faults one to another, and pray one for another, that ye may be healed. The effectual fervent prayer of a righteous man availeth much. We need to rely on one another to hold us accountable for our actions. You know all this kind behavior is not of God this is just another trick of the enemy. We know he doesn't have any new ones, so he just mixes his little bag of tricks up and pull out something a different way to entice us and make us fall short of God's glory. He is just doing his job that's his calling. The key is not to let him take you out of the will of God and what you're called to do.

These types of behaviors are can appear to be subtle and may not be obvious to the natural eye at first glance, but the Spirit can detect the foul odors in the air. Leaders may try to hide in the church amongst other leaders but eventually, who you are and what you do, will eventually be exposed. Remember we serve a just God! These behaviors always start out so innocently and some just error but can grow to be destructive to the Body of Christ if we don't remain humble and integral. To whom much is given much is required, but some leaders can't handle the "much" part. It's kind of like winning the lottery. If you come from a disadvantage background where you may have not been as fortunate to have had a lot of wealth in your home or environment and you win the lottery. If you don't get guidance, direction and help from someone who is experience in handling that type of wealth, you won't know how to handle it. It will change you on every level, for better or for the worst. It will question your character, integrity, values, and challenge your behavior and eventually kill your spirit and if you don't know, or don't want to know. Some leaders do a lot of dirt behind closed doors and have shown no remorse for it. We walk around with the notion that I'm always right. News Flash! you are not always right, but in due season the spotlight will shine on you if you don't get it right.

The bible says when you sin, it's only against God that you sin. God see's everything. Did you forget He is omnipresent? Time get it together leaders before your time runs out. You know I'm talking right. You've seen Him do it in our lifetime. People are watching us and we need to be an example to the Body of Christ. Some other leaders extort money from people, asking for ten different offerings. We are asked to pay for "prophe-lies", and you know you made that up or somebody told you their business. Yes, you know who you are. We want to have total control over people lives. We want to tell grown people who they can and cannot talk to. We manipulate their time, keep them in church all day, every day, all kinds of hours, with no consideration for the lives they have. We try to brainwash people using scriptures incorrectly and all out of context. Ya'll know what I'm talking about, need I say more. You know who you are and what damage you've done, it's not right so fix it or God will. Psalms 44:21 says He knoweth the secrets of the heart, you can't hide your sinful ways, and you know the heart is desperately wicked. A cruel you plus a wicked heart equals danger and destruction.

When you have "Greed" you have that intense and selfish desire for something, especially wealth and power that is never quenched. The more you get, the more you want, and from anybody you can manipulate to get it, by any means necessary. When you aim to "control" someone you want that power that will influence or direct people's behavior or the course of events to whatever way you want that benefits you and if you don't get your way, all involved have hell to pay, yes I said it, hell to pay.

Then here comes "pride", which is like an addiction. You need that feeling of deep pleasure or satisfaction to achieve and accomplish what you want in someone else or something else but it's always about you. This prideful behavior has a few names. It's also described as conceit, egotism, and vanity, vainglory, all over one's own appearance or status in life and not just something that's been accomplished. Guess what? It gives you that feeling of being high and it always show up before the fall but if you're blessed enough, you can catch yourself.

I believe, from what I've read in the Bible, that pride is at the root of all sin. God hates pride because it's really a misplaced sense of worth. Now let's go back over each and back it up with scripture.

Pride- God says that "In his pride the wicked man does not seek him; in all his thoughts there is no room for God" (Psalm 10:4). I hate pride and arrogance, evil behavior and perverse speech" (Proverbs 8:13). When pride comes, then comes disgrace, but with humility comes wisdom. Proverbs 11:2 Now when James writes that "God opposes the proud but gives grace to the humble" (James 4:6). I want to be humble. God hates pride and we are supposed to hate what He hates and love what He loves. You see the world operates from a sense of pride and it is not of God. This is what the Apostle John wrote in 1st John 2:16 "For everything in the world—the lust of the flesh, the lust of the eyes, and the pride of life—comes not from the Father but from the world" which is exactly what happened to Satan and caused the fall of Adam and Eve in the Garden. The way of Edom is the way that most of the world operates as Obadiah writes "The pride of your heart has deceived you, you who live in the clefts of the rocks and make your home on the heights, you who say to yourself, 'Who can bring me down to the ground" (Obadiah 1:3). So, pride can severely deceive us. It can make you think you are so much more than you are. Remember the same thing happened to King Belshazzar "when his heart became arrogant and hardened with pride, he was deposed from his royal throne and stripped of his glory" (Dan 5:20). Ooowee! To be stripped of God's glory, who wants that? Don't you know what the glory brings it's not just a part of God; it is God and all that He is. Who in their right mind would want to forfeit this privilege? Well the King did, and many leaders have also done it as well. The glory is not about, riches power or material beauty, it's all about God.

Now let's talk about greed--- Luke 12:15 Then he said to them, "Watch out! Be on your guard against all kinds of greed; a man's life does not consist in the abundance of his possessions. 1 Corinthians 6:10 says nor thieves nor the greedy nor drunkards nor slanderers nor swindlers will inherit the kingdom of God. Why forfeit what God has for you because of greed. Don't you know he is the source of everything and the creator all it all. Ask, seek and Knock for it, stop being a thief. That's Satan thang.

And then there's Control, Control. 2nd Tim 3:1-5 says "But, understand this, that in the last days there will come times of difficulty. For people will be lovers of self, lovers of money, proud, arrogant, abusive, and disobedient to their parents, ungrateful, unholy, heartless, unappeasable, and slanderous, without self-control, brutal, not loving good, treacherous, reckless, and swollen with conceit, lovers of pleasure rather than lovers of God.

Having the appearance of godliness but denying its power. Avoid such people, get away from them, and don't let bad company corrupt you." Don't be deceived these are those last days spoken and written in the bible, just look around you and open your eyes; this is what's already happening to some of us leaders in the Body of Christ we already walking in this thing and we think it's alright but it's not.

I'm done! That's all I got to say because God has the final say. Repent while you still have time. Lord Help us not to fall.

Scriptures

Hebrews 4:13 – *"Nothing in all creation is hidden from God's sight. Everything is uncovered and laid bare before the eyes of him to whom we must give account."*

Psalm 90:8 – *"You have set our iniquities before you, our secret sins in the light of your presence"*

Ecclesiastes 12:14 – *"For God will bring every deed into judgment, including every hidden thing, whether it is good or evil."*

Romans 2:16 – *tells us "God will judge men's secrets through Jesus Christ."*

I Corinthians 4:5 – *"He will bring to light what is hidden in darkness and will expose the motives of men's hearts."*

Ephesians 5:12 - *(Message Bible) It's a scandal when people waste their lives on things they must do in the darkness where no one will see.*

Prayer

Lord, I repent of my sins. Wash me with hyssop; against you only have I done these deeds. Forgive me, change my heart change my mind, create in me a clean heart and all that is desperately wicked, expose it and remove it. Get my spirit right Lord, and please allow those that I have wronged and did these things against help them to forgive me and help me to make it right with them. Thank you for pulling me out of the pit of destruction. Make me self-aware of my evil ways and fix me Lord. Change me and bring me back to my first love that is you, your people, and the church ministry that you gave me and who you trusted me with. Lord, thank you for covering me and not exposing me, thank you for catching me before the fall. Remove this destructive combination out of my spirit. Remove Greed, remove control, and remove pride now. In Jesus name!

OBSERVATION TWENTY-ONE

Is it Five-Fold, Three-fold, Two-Fold or One-fold Ministry?

Are we all reading the same Bible? the Holy Bible, La Biblia, the Holy Writ, the Good book, the Book of all Books? I'm conf®used, then why do we only choose to adhere to certain scriptures. I never understood that and probably never will. It just doesn't make sense to me. Now with that said, let's take a look at this scripture in Ephesians. What is a swelling church? - A swelling church is what grows in width and houses a lot of unused gifts. All the gifts and talents are stuck on the inside and nothing ever goes out. It swells and stretches until it can't anymore and eventually it explodes and bursts, and the people scatter and go other places so they can grow and use their gifts. ~ the author, me.

Ephesians 4:11-16 King James Version (KJV)

[11] And he gave some, apostles; and some, prophets; and some, evangelists; and some, pastors and teachers;

[12] For the perfecting of the saints, for the work of the ministry, for the edifying of the body of Christ:

[13] Till we all come in the unity of the faith, and of the knowledge of the Son of God, unto a perfect man, unto the measure of the stature of the fullness of Christ:

[14] That we henceforth be no more children, tossed to and fro, and carried about with every wind of doctrine, by the sleight of men, and cunning craftiness, whereby they lie in wait to deceive;

[15] but speaking the truth in love, may grow up into him in all things, which is the head, even Christ:

[16] from whom the whole body fitly joined together and compacted by that which every joint supplieth, according to the effectual working in the measure of every part, maketh increase of the body unto the edifying of itself in love.

The word clearly states that He gave some apostles and some prophets and some evangelist and pastors and teachers. So how can the Body of Christ only have deacons and ministers in a church with over 5,000 members and over 300-500 leaders in the church and only have evangelist, deacons and or missionaries and evangelist. Now there is no way that there are no prophets, no teachers, no evangelists with gifting that exist in your house...just pastors. The bible clearly states that there is more, and somebody's gift is lying dormant and not being used because leaders fail to recognize it. Do leaders just choose to not recognize this order or are we afraid of the gifts? Or is religion and tradition a big part of our why? My take is that we are afraid of the gifts and what the prophet might say about you and the direction of the church. Or that the teacher might know more than you and teach the people a good word and gain their respect and make you feel envious.

I've seen it and I've been on the end of this spectrum. Let me give you an example. God gave me a prophetic word to give to the Pastors, I respectfully asked to speak to them privately gave the word, one of the Pastors was on board the other turned up their nose, but it didn't matter because he was the Bishop of the church, I was going to be obedient to God whether the word was received or not. The next day the Bishop came to me and gave me instructions and told me to, pray and whatever God says bring it back to him. I guess God had a chat with him in the midnight hour. I did what he said he implemented what God told me to bring back and it all came to pass, and the church thrived, and God got the glory. Remember, I said only one pastor was on board so as the prophecy unfolded the other pastor and their followers of leaders began to treat me badly and ostracize me, etc. Remember, I was a leader to at that church.

Well you know how that story went, but I was created for "THIS" and the adversity and persecution that comes along. I am a prophet of order, who tears down governmental traps and structure in the church. I am one who shines the light on tradition and religious man-made structure built to enslave the people in the church. Well after being in the church for a while, I had deep yearning although I knew I was just passing through because it was so much more on the inside that God put in me. Once I was trained in the area in which that church was excellently operating in, I was preparing for God to move me so I could grow. My prayer was always Lord please don't let my gift and talents die in a church.

Okay, so if this is not happening, how are the saints getting perfected? How is the body being edified and how are the full works of the ministry are being established? Is it only through Pastor and Leader, and only the gift you possess is thriving, being used, and growing?

Listen Leaders, we hinder what God is trying to do in our midst and in the Body of Christ when we don't follow the word of God and recognize all the gifts that are in your house, you don't get to just pick two gifts that you want to use or operate. You are doing your Church a disservice for where God is trying to take you. I've seen this operation go on for years. What do you do when your teaching and training no longer fills the needs of the people who have these gifts that lay dormant inside of them, and only recognize a few that you're decided to recognize as long as they are not larger or exceed your title? Oh, oh, I just said something right there. Well you know what happens you stop growing, the people stop growing, and the church is left standing still. But because it's business as usual, you think you're moving forward but you really are standing still.

What should take the church 3 or 4 years to accomplish, will take 10-12, or until you submit to the will of God! Stop hindering the blessing that God wants to bestow upon your ministry. People are waiting for you to grow-up in your region. Yes, people you never met with gifts on top of gifts, sons and daughter who are going to travel around the world with the fivefold ministry gifts representing you. Now as a church and your people have stopped growing because you limit your church to what God has in mind for them to do. Now some of leaders have taken them as far as they can go because they are supposed to open churches, be Pastors, lead sheep, Evangelize, teach and go out to the nations. You should have sent out tons of leaders to build and start new churches under your leadership by now, but you haven't sent out one because you're selfish and want to keep them in your church. May the Lord have mercy on your soul. It's sad that you can't take them into this purpose or to that next level, and you have the nerve and audacity to get angry or upset when the spirit of the Lord is moving in their life and the unction of the Holy spirit is pushing them out and they leave the ministry to fulfill the call that God has placed on their life. Stop getting mad someone had to let you go to fulfill their calling. Yes, some just leave abruptly and some leave in order, but because you are not accepting the letter to resign or won't see them and sit down to talk with them and pronounce a blessing over them, well that's on you! Remember, I am speaking from experience not what I heard.

Most of the Churches are swelling in growth but not getting tall in height. (Oh, you'll get that one later) Remember I gave the definition in the beginning of this Observation. The people are spiritually dying. Please take time to exam your ministry, survey your leaders ask them what gifts they believe God has bestow on them and use your discernment and prayer life to weed them out, because the wheat does grow with the tares. As an Apostle, Bishop and Pastor of a congregation, not wanting to recognize gifts, talents and abilities but only recognizing these certain gifts, tells me something about you as a leader. Maybe you have not fully tapped into your own gifts of what God has placed inside of you! And if you don't acknowledge and tap into the gifts that you have you won't be able to recognize the gifting on the future leaders in your congregation. If we know better, we need to do better at least we're supposed to. Yes, I have been a part of a ministry like this and the sad part is this ministry could be huge birthing out leaders all over the world, but they refuse to change. Let's go back to this question; what are we truly afraid of? Is it exposure that someone may know a little bit more than you? Is it that you think they're going to take your place or replace your truth? They will respect you more and claim you as their covering and spiritual parents as they grow and go. They will probably honor you more for helping them to grow to the next level, so what is it? Open your minds and your heart and watch God do wonders. Let the prophets prophesy, the evangelist evangelize, and let the teachers teach, and birth out the Pastors.

I've seen pastors come from all over to the church, ordained and licensed and proven, and you tell them their license is no good here they have to start over. You don't get to strip them of their titles or ignore them when they bring it to your attention. Who do you think you are? God was sending you help, and I've seen this so many times done right. Put them on trial, give them training to learn the culture of the church, verify their credentials, and put them to work. Train the Pastors to do greater works for the glory of God. They are not leaving because they want to, they are just frustrated and tired sitting when they can see all the gaps in the church and want to assist you in the ministry, that's all.

Scriptures

Ephesians: 4:11 – *"And he gave some, apostles; and some, prophets; and some, evangelists; and some, pastors and teachers;"*

Prayer

Father, help me to abide by your word, as you said to Peter "if you love me, then feed my sheep." Help me to establish the church as your desire and build leaders according to your will. Help me feed your sheep and the members that make up the body. Help me and teach me to recognize what you have given us in the church so I may cultivate those gifts. Lord where I am lacking and neglected some gifts within me and bring them forth that I may nurture the congregation that you've place in my hand and under my care. Cast out fear, jealousy and envy. Search my heart concerning these matters and make it clean. In Jesus name I pray. Amen

THE CONCLUSION OF THE MATTER

Let me start off with my disclaimer. I know this book was not popular for some to read, and a little painful and uncomfortable for others. But if you know me, you know I heard God through fasting and prayer and I'm obedient to his instructions. Bottom line is God gave it to me to do and I said, "Yes". Remember this is what He allowed me to see and experience my almost 20 years of serving in ministry. I'm that one, and that prophet that will confront system and structures in the church. God conditioned me for this over the years so I can take the hit for any opposition that may be received if need be.When I was going through it, it didn't feel good, I thought I was crazy with what I was seeing and feeling. I was disappointed, and at times I was sad and thought I wanted to die for the depths of what I had experienced. Everything I've experienced was for my good and everything I was exposed to was necessary. These things catapulted me into ministry, strengthen and developed my prayer life, and gave me clarity in hearing God's voice. My ability to fast was enhanced. It sharpened my discernment and gave me the boldness I needed to prophesy, lay hands and intercede for others. It taught me forgiveness and grace at a whole different level. It's the suffering and the hurt that builds you and where you grow the most. And that's the place where God can really use you the most. Most of all it taught me to love and love unconditionally. One thing I know for sure is that through it all, He was with me every step of the way. Though He slay me yet will I trust him. God used me and all of my experiences to bring others out and save souls and for that I'm grateful that He saw fit to use me for His glory.

Why now? because God said so, I been trying to birth this book out for two years, but God kept saying no, not yet and He would freeze my thoughts and I would move on to something else. To write a book as such takes a certain kind of an anointing – one that He has conditioned me for over the years.

I love God, I love the church, and I love His people. I love the sinner but hate the sin. It is said that the state of the church is dead. There is cult activity in the church and the spirit of seduction and intimidation has taken over, and the church is out of control. The world is laughing and refuses to grace us with their presence. As leaders, we have pushed people out of the Church with our behavior and God said He is truly not pleased, and this is His clarion call for us as leaders to get it together repent and get back to holiness and righteousness. If you notice throughout the book, I'm not attempting to point the finger at anyone in particular. You know your faults. You know your sins. I'm letting spirit do the convicting. Just to let you know, I'm in the fight to see us win as leaders and that's why I used words like we, us, ours and all because I too am a leader; one who grieves for the Body of Christ.

We are building new church buildings and the ones we're in have not been fixed. Do we really think God is going to ordain a bigger mess? Not so! Repent and go back to your first love. I remember there was a time and an era where God was building Mega Churches everywhere and the houses where being filled to capacity. But now-a-days, you don't see many Mega churches going up anymore and the ones that are up have already been established for years. What I see God doing is going back to the small church concept where the intimate setting is necessary to get His Word out and change lives. I am not saying that's not happening in the Mega Churches, but in the mega church the people can hide and never get noticed, and the Pastor will never know their name or who they are or the gifts they have if they never come forth. But in the smaller churches, you are easy detected and exposed. When the atmosphere is smaller and more intimate you can be discovered and made to grow.

Fortunately for us grace still abounds, the gospel will still be preached in the church according to Philippians 1:17-19 (NLT)

> [17] *Those others do not have pure motives as they preach about Christ. They preach with selfish ambition, not sincerely, intending to make my chains more painful to me.* [18] *But that doesn't matter. Whether their motives are false or genuine, the message about Christ is being preached either way, so I rejoice. And I will continue to rejoice.* [19] *For I know that as you pray for me and the Spirit of Jesus Christ helps me, this will lead to my deliverance.*

I stand on the word of God and speak with authority according to Act 18:9-10 (NLT) [9] *One night the Lord spoke to Paul in a vision and told him, "Don't be afraid! Speak out! Don't be silent!* [10] *For I am with you, and no one will attack and harm you, for many people in this city belong to me."*

Psalms 105:14-15 - *He allowed no one to oppress them; for their sake he rebuked kings:*

"Do not touch my anointed ones; do my prophets no harm."

Touch not my anointed and do my prophet no harm. Remember as leaders we are not the only ones anointed and for the record, I too am anointed and a prophet of God. SELAH.

And my final question is what are you? A good shepherd or a hireling?

I am not going to say too much about this but I will let the scripture speak for itself as you ponder and think on these things. Take time to exam yourself and your behavior, and as Leaders we should ask ourselves; I'm a good Shepherd or a hireling? What's my behavior been like? How do others see me and not how I see myself? Truth be told, how great you see yourself, isn't necessarily how great others always see you. Have an accountability person -- someone that will tell you the truth and not be afraid to do so, not a yes man or yes women, who fear you or fears retaliation from you. Remember people are looking at everything: your good, your bad and your ugly...and especially when you're always acting real ugly. You know the church and the world likes a good drama story. Yes, you still have sheep obeying you, most of the time but they are tolerating you and not celebrating you. Some are thinking internally and are in waiting to hear the voice of God to move or go on the next assignment. It's a bad feeling to come to Church and be mistreated by your leaders and leave feeling gutted, like you never should have been there. Some people have endured the pressures of life all week and look forward to that place where they can find refuge, worship and an outpouring of love and the spirit of the Lord. Imagine being so disappointed. You have been there... yeah you... oh how soon we forget. And then again, we know how it feels, so why would we want to allow someone to endure that same ole pain? Stop playing the victim always saying "the sheep did this to me and the sheep did that to me". It's not personal... it comes with the call.

Let me say this: God has sent you some leaders that may have been previously at a place that they were overlooked or just used for their gifts and was not being trained properly. Well this has happened more times than most. A lot of times that person came to you to learn and grow and at the same time, God simultaneously places them in that Church to help the Church and to see if He can trust you with them without implementing your selfish agenda. Well if they are faithful in whatever position they are in, then eventually God will move them because they have achieved what they were sent to accomplish. Sometimes that is the farthest those Pastors are able to take them, based on the power and anointing God has bestowed upon that ministry. Now God sends them to your Ministry because He trusts that you can handle the anointing on their life. You can train them and teach them as God has directed you to do. Then you pray to hear from God, and you elevate them to their prospective place. But somewhere in the process they may do something to offend you or disappoint you and you bring up the fact that the ministry they came from didn't do anything for them and when they got to your ministry. You elevated them, so you remind them every time when something goes wrong or even go right. Why is that? Is it because now you are holding that over their heads, and you feel they owe you and you want them to be indebted to you for life? But what happen to the part that through pray God told you to elevate them? Or did you just elevate them out of your emotion because you wanted them to be indebted to you and stay at the church, or was that a lie and promotion came from you and not God? Well if God said it, then they owe you nothing. Again, they don't owe you anything. They owe God everything. God used you as a vessel. He entrusted them in your care so, that you could do the right thing by them based on your experience and knowledge that He has put in you to build His Kingdom, so stop putting that burden on their heads and in their hearts unless you deceived them.

For promotion cometh neither from the east, nor from the west, nor from the south.

But God is the judge: he putteth down one, and setteth up another. For in the hand of the LORD there is a cup, and the wine is red; it is full of mixture; and he poureth out of the same: but the dregs thereof, all the wicked of the earth shall wring them out, and drink them.

Don't abort the mission

Think on these things. Scriptures to meditate on:

JOHN 10 (NKJV)
Jesus the True Shepherd

[1] *"Most assuredly, I say to you, he who does not enter the sheepfold by the door, but climbs up some other way, the same is a thief and a robber. [2] But he who enters by the door is the shepherd of the sheep. [3] To him the doorkeeper opens, and the sheep hear his voice; and he calls his own sheep by name and leads them out. [4] And when*

he brings out his own sheep, he goes before them; and the sheep follow him, for they know his voice. *⁵ Yet they will by no means follow a stranger, but will flee from him, for they do not know the voice of strangers." ⁶ Jesus used this illustration, but they did not understand the things which He spoke to them.*

Jesus the Good Shepherd

⁷ Then Jesus said to them again, "Most assuredly, I say to you, I am the door of the sheep. ⁸ All who ever came before Me are thieves and robbers, but the sheep did not hear them. ⁹ I am the door. If anyone enters by Me, he will be saved, and will go in and out and find pasture. ¹⁰ The thief does not come except to steal, and to kill, and to destroy. I have come that they may have life, and that they may have it more abundantly.

¹¹ "I am the good shepherd. The good shepherd gives His life for the sheep. ¹² But a hireling, he who is not the shepherd, one who does not own the sheep, sees the wolf coming and leaves the sheep and flees; and the wolf catches the sheep and scatters them. ¹³ The hireling flees because he is a hireling and does not care about the sheep. ¹⁴ I am the good shepherd; and I know My sheep, and am known by My own. ¹⁵ As the Father knows Me, even so I know the Father; and I lay down My life for the sheep. ¹⁶ And other sheep I have which are not of this fold; them also I must bring, and they will hear My voice; and there will be one flock and one shepherd.

¹⁷ "Therefore My Father loves Me, because I lay down My life that I may take it again. ¹⁸ No one takes it from Me, but I lay it down of Myself. I have power to lay it down, and I have power to take it again. This command I have received from My Father." ¹⁹ Therefore there was a division again among the Jews because of these sayings. ²⁰ And many of them said, "He has a demon and is mad. Why do you listen to Him?" [21] Others said, "These are not the words of one who has a demon. Can a demon open the eyes of the blind?"

The Shepherd Knows His Sheep

[22] Now it was the Feast of Dedication in Jerusalem, and it was winter. [23] And Jesus walked in the temple, in Solomon's porch. [24] Then the Jews surrounded Him and said to Him, "How long do You keep us in doubt? If You are the Christ, tell us plainly."

[25] Jesus answered them, "I told you, and you do not believe. The works that I do in My Father's name, they bear witness of Me. [26] But you do not believe, because you are not of My sheep as I said to you. [27] My sheep hear My voice, and I know them, and they follow Me. [28] And I give them eternal life, and they shall never perish; neither shall anyone snatch them out of My hand. [29] My Father, who has given them to Me, is greater than all; and no one is able to snatch them out of My Father's hand. [30] I and My Father are one."

Renewed Efforts to Stone Jesus

[31] Then the Jews took up stones again to stone Him. [32] Jesus answered them, "Many good works I have shown you from My Father. For which of those works do you stone Me?"

[33] The Jews answered Him, saying, "For a good work we do not stone You, but for blasphemy, and because You, being a Man, make Yourself God."

[34] Jesus answered them, "Is it not written in your law, 'I said, "You are gods"'? [35] If He called them gods, to whom the word of God came (and the Scripture cannot be broken), [36] do you say of Him whom the Father sanctified and sent into the world, 'You are blaspheming,' because I said, 'I am the Son of God'? [37] If I do not do the works of My Father, do not believe Me; [38] but if I do, though you do not

believe Me, believe the works, that you may know and believe that the Father is in Me, and I in Him."³⁹ Therefore they sought again to seize Him, but He escaped out of their hand.

The Believers Beyond Jordan

⁴⁰ And He went away again beyond the Jordan to the place where John was baptizing at first, and there He stayed. ⁴¹ Then many came to Him and said, "John performed no sign, but all the things that John spoke about this Man were true." ⁴² And many believed in Him there.

Scriptures

Lord, forgive me if I have mishandled the gift that you put in my care. I'm sorry for making myself lord over your people and using that against them and to work in my favor! You are Lord over everything, and promotion and elevation come from you and you only.

May the grace of the Lord Jesus be with you and God's people.